THE ENCYCLOPEDIA OF
WIRE JEWELRY
TECHNIQUES

THE ENCYCLOPEDIA OF
WIRE JEWELRY TECHNIQUES

A compendium of step-by-step techniques for making wire-based jewelry

SARA WITHERS

WITH XUELLA ARNOLD AND ELISE MANN

RUNNING PRESS
PHILADELPHIA • LONDON

A QUARTO BOOK

First published in the United States in
2010 by Running Press Book Publishers.
First paperback edition published in 2011.

10 9 8 7 6 5 4 3 2 1
Digit on the right indicates the number
of this printing.

Conceived, designed, and produced by
Quarto Publishing plc
The Old Brewery
6 Blundell Street
London N7 9BH

QUAR.WJT

ISBN-13: 978-0-7624-4577-6

Library of Congress Cataloging-in-
Publication Data available on request

Senior editor: Ruth Patrick
Art editor: Emma Clayton
Art director: Caroline Guest
Designers: Julie Francis. Karin Skanberg
Photographer: Simon Pask
Illustrator: Kuo Kang Chen
Picture researcher: Sarah Bell

Creative director: Moira Clinch
Publisher: Paul Carslake

Color separation in China by Modern
  Age Pte Ltd
Printed in China by 1010 Printing
  International Ltd

Running Press Book Publishers
2300 Chestnut Street
Philadelphia, Pennsylvania 19103-4371
Visit us on the web!
www.runningpress.com

Contents

Wire-wrapped marble on a
thong decorated with coils.

Introduction

The enjoyment of beads and jewelry-making is a progressive process. It begins with finding a few beads that you like and wondering what you can do with them. Or you might admire a piece of jewelry and wonder if you could make something like that for yourself. It's a process that seems to have been happening for thousands of years!

Nowadays anyone who gets interested in jewelry-making has a choice of routes that they can follow. You can perfect your stringing and knotting skills, develop your beadworking techniques so that you know how to use all the tiny delica and rocaille beads found in bead shops, head off to silversmithing classes, or learn more about wire.

The purpose of this book is to explain and demystify the different functions of jewelry-making wires and to take you through the basic techniques that will enable you to build your wire skills. We will take you through the experience of working with wire from the most simple pair of earrings, to making your own findings and chains and being able to decorate and use a found object, such as a pebble or seaglass that doesn't have a hole in it.

To make the book as comprehensive as possible, a section has been created, with the help of co-authors, that initiates you into the complex use of jump rings so that you can learn to make chains or "chain mail." Another section introduces you to silversmithing techniques so that you know what the next steps can be with silver or gold wires if you start to use heating and soldering techniques.

SARA WITHERS

Tools

You either already have or will very quickly assemble a set of your favorite tools, and you'll probably also find ones that work for you that aren't featured here.

A few pointers

Always work with plenty of wire—you will hurt your hands if you work with short pieces. It is often a good idea to develop your designs using an inexpensive plated wire rather than working with precious wires and worrying about spoiling them.

Until you get to the Toward silversmithing section (see page 118), these are all techniques that you can work on at your kitchen table, but do make sure that you work in a good light. Take care of yourself as you work; wear safety glasses or learn to control the wire that you are cutting so that you don't have small pieces going into your eyes.

Remember that you will develop your own interpretations of the techniques shown when you become more skillful. Most people work in slightly different ways, for example many jewelry makers make the closed loops shown on page 18 by using two pairs of pliers. The enjoyment in learning the techniques is in discovering how you can make them work for you so that you enjoy creating your own designs.

> TIP **Don't use your best wire cutters to cut the nylon-coated beading wires as these will blunt them. Also make sure that you use slightly heavier cutters for heavier jewelry-making wires.**

Basic tools

1 ROUND-NOSE PLIERS

You will need a good, neat pair of round-nose pliers that fit comfortably into the palm of your hand and have delicate "noses."

2 CHAIN-NOSE PLIERS

Chain- or snipe-nose pliers are essential for most of the basics. Again you need their "noses" to be neat. Make sure that all your pliers have smooth surfaces on the insides of their noses.

3 WIRE CUTTERS

This is a tool that you really need to focus on. Choose ones with really pointed ends so that you can get closely into your work.

MORE TOOLS

Once you have your basic tools, you can begin to collect all your other favorite tools. Your choice will depend on which techniques you choose to specialize in.

4 WIDE-NOSE PLIERS

These will help you with heavier wires and for larger-scale work. They are particularly useful when working with stiff jump rings.

5 ACRYLIC-NOSE PLIERS

If you are working with colored wires, these pliers will help to prevent you marking the wires. They are also helpful with all wires as you can run the pliers down them to remove any kinks and strengthen them.

6 HAMMER AND BLOCK

A hammer is extremely useful and doesn't need to be bought from a specialist supplier. A block is helpful too. You could use an old iron or other smooth metal surface, but a proper block isn't expensive and, for the sort of work that you will be doing with wire, you will only need a small one.

7 FILES

These are essential whenever you need a smooth end to your wire. Look for quite fine ones.

8 CUP BURR

You will need to go to a specialist supplier for this. A cup burr is a very good tool if you are making earwires as it smoothes the end of a piece of wire, and can remove the need for files.

9 BENT-NOSE PLIERS

These are useful if you are working a lot with jump rings.

10 PIN VISE

This is a helpful tool if you want to twist two wires together or twist a square wire to create a twisted one.

11 GIZMO

A great way to make spirals of wire quickly—you can make very decorative beads with a Gizmo.

12 JIG

This tool is good if you want to make lots of decorative spacers as it enables you to make several identical pieces. You can now get a tool that makes coils with the jig.

13 RING MANDREL

This allows you to work out the sizes of rings and create the correct-size shaft. If you want to make only a few rings, you can probably manage with other tubular objects.

14 MEMORY WIRE CUTTERS

These are very heavy-duty cutters and are essential if you want to work with a lot of memory wire, which will ruin other wire cutters. They are also useful for other very heavy wires.

Household items

It is amazing how many times you will find exactly what you need lying around in the house —ballpoint pens and marker pens are invaluable and you will find yourself wrapping wire around many other items that come to hand. The potential uses of everyday items can be surprising—you can even use hard-boiled eggs if you wish to oxidize (darken) the silver wires that you have worked with.

TAPE MEASURE OR RULER

Remember that you will want to keep a record of the lengths of wire that you need for different designs. It is always a good idea to keep a "master" length of wire to work from so that you can measure others against it. But a tape measure or a ruler is also a great help.

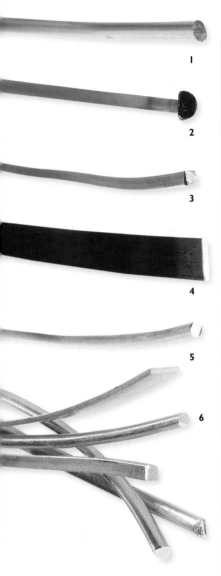

1 Oval wire

2 D-shaped wire

3 Square wire

4 Rectangular wire

5 Round wire

6 Assorted wires

Materials

There are so many different types of wire available now that it is almost possible to be spoilt for choice.

Types of wire

Some of the projects in this book have been made with silver plate jewelry wire. This has a copper core and is very easy to use, which makes it an excellent choice to practice with. Many colored wires have also been used; some of these hold their color very well but others mark more easily. When you become more experienced, there are more precious wires available such as sterling silver or gold wires that you can try. You will need to use these for any findings that are to go through your ears.

Wire classifications

You need to be aware of both the sizes that are used to categorize wire and the degree of their hardness. It was once reasonably simple to calculate the thickness of your wire—in Britain the size was marked in millimeters (usually rounded down to keep it simple), while in the United States a gauge system was used—the AWG (American Wire Gauge). So a medium thickness wire is referred to as a 22 gauge or 0.6 mm wire. However, some suppliers use the Standard Wire Gauge, which is different from AWG. It is important to be confident about the diameters of your wires in millimeters and to be aware that the AWG sizes work on a scale in which the higher numbers represent the finer wires. The sizes of wires given in the techniques in this book have been specified first in AWG and then in millimeters. The table opposite will help you to learn these. Remember to use wires that are strong enough for the job that you need them to do.

    The next consideration is which hardness of wire to choose. Sterling and gold wires can be bought in five grades of hardness from 0, which is very soft, to 4, which is fully hardened. For most wirework you will work in soft or half-hard wire. You will need a soft grade when you are working with heavier wires to enable you to manipulate them without the need to heat them. Half-hard wire is a good crisp wire that keeps its shape very well and is easy to use.

    Silver plate wires in 22 gauge (0.6 mm) and 20 gauge (0.8 mm) behave very like their equivalents in sterling silver and will give you a good feeling for them. Precious wires can also be bought in different shapes such as square and half-round.

    When you are choosing jump rings they are usually measured by internal diameter and wire thickness. Different thicknesses of wire

Reels of silver and copper wire.

Reels of colored wire.

Jump rings in assorted sizes made from various wires.

are suitable for different chain patterns. Be aware that, for their size, thinner jump rings will make a looser, less stable chain, so if you use larger rings they will need to be proportionally thicker to ensure a firm, neat look. Rings in which the wire is too thick for the pattern will prevent the chain from bending in a fluid fashion.

You will be able to buy your wires and jump rings from many different sources, including bead shops and online suppliers.

Don't forget the other, more unusual wires that you may be able to use, such as brightly colored electrical wires or the new ready-knitted wires that are now available.

WIRE GAUGE CHART

Gauge	Diameter in AWG	Diameter in SWG
16	1.30 mm	1.63 mm
18	1.02 mm	1.22 mm
20	0.81 mm	0.91 mm
21*	0.73 mm	0.81 mm
22	0.63 mm	0.71 mm
24	0.50 mm	0.55 mm
26	0.40 mm	0.45 mm
28	0.32 mm	0.37 mm
30	0.25 mm	0.31 mm

* This gauge of wire is often used to make earwires.

TIP **Remember that the AWG size is usually rounded up or down— 20 gauge becomes 0.8 mm and 22 gauge becomes 0.6 mm. This simplified measurement style is used throughout the book.**

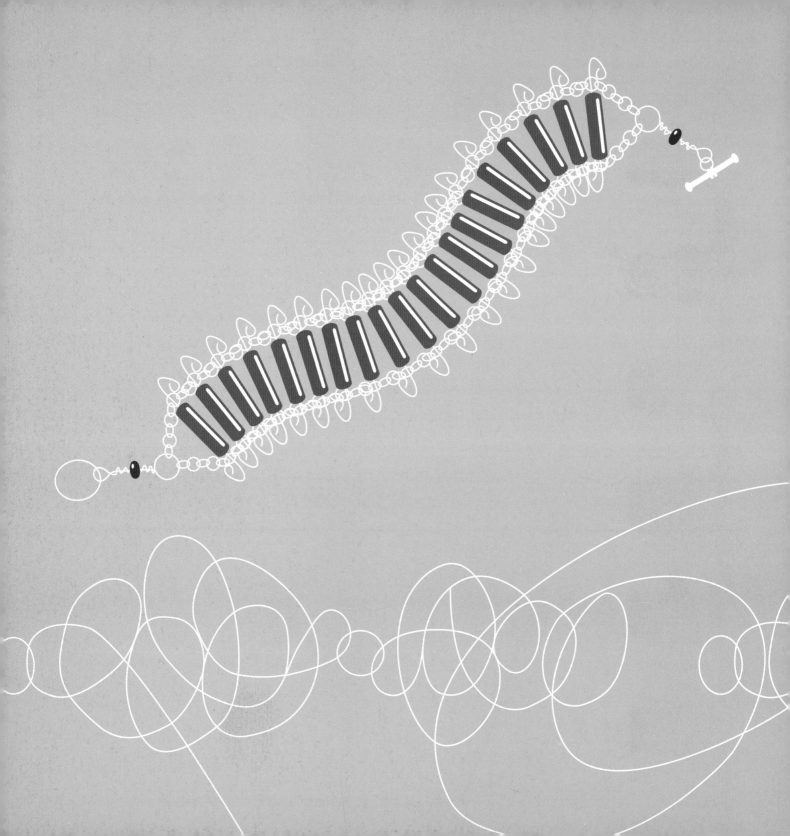

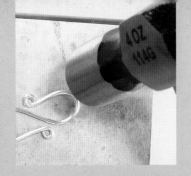

CHAPTER ONE

Core Techniques

This chapter covers the core techniques of working with wire in jewelry making. Starting with the basic building blocks, such as how to handle your tools and wires, the basic techniques that you will do time and again are covered, then ideas are given for findings and chains. Basic knitting and twisting techniques are included, followed by ideas for decorating stones and beads, and moving into providing a groundwork for creating bangles, rings, and brooches.

Wire basics

These are a few very basic techniques that you need to remember when working your way through this book.

Holding pliers

It is important to hold your pliers firmly and to to be comfortable with them. Use your finger and thumb to control one side of the pliers and your other fingers to control the other side.

Strengthening wire

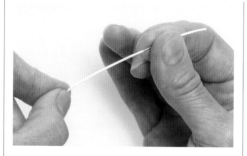

It is a good idea to run your fingers or a pair of pliers down the wire as you work. This will strengthen and "work-harden" the wire by activating the properties of the metal.

If you are working with expensive wires you will save a lot by running acrylic-nose pliers down them to remove kinks. Remember that if you overwork your wires they can become "fatigued" and will then break.

Cutting wire

Always cut your wire with the flat side of the wire cutters facing the side of the wire that you are creating, not the piece of wire that you are going to discard.

TIP **Always be very careful when you are cutting or handling wire. Wear safety glasses for complete protection and be careful that any small pieces of wire don't go into your eyes or those of anyone near you. The ends of wire can also be very sharp, especially the memory wire shown on page 96. You will be safer, and hurt your hands less, if you work with generous amounts of wire. Finally, don't forget that some of your tools are sharp.**

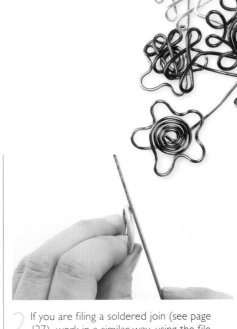

Filing

1 | If possible, you should always file any end of wire that isn't going to be tucked away against a bead. Work around the wire, directing the file away from you.

2 | If you are filing a soldered join (see page 127), work in a similar way, using the file in one direction rather than backward and forward.

3 | Work round the contours of the piece that you are making with lots of gentle movements.

Using a cup burr

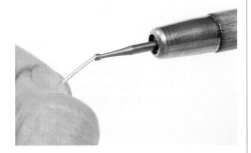

Another tool to try when you need to smooth the end of a piece of wire, especially when working on earwires, is a cup burr. Fit your wire inside the tip of a cup burr and twist it around for a smooth finish.

Opening loops

When you have created a loop in a finding, or if you are using ready-made findings, always open the loop sideways so that you don't spoil the shape.

Opening jump rings

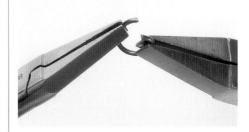

Jump rings should be opened sideways too. With heavy-gauge jump rings you can use two pairs of pliers to move the sides apart. Some jump rings are designed to be moved sideways a couple of times until you get a really tight join.

Using ready-made findings

This book will teach you to use wire in many different ways, including making some of your own findings (see page 26). But you can gain confidence with wire first by using some ready-made findings.

Headpins and eyepins come in many different lengths, thicknesses, and finishes. Headpins have flat ends and eyepins have a small loop at one end—your choice will be dependent on the look that you want to achieve. Eyepins are useful if you want to link two lengths together. For earring making, thin, hard headpins and eyepins are generally easier to use than soft ones.

Earwires also come in many different types. It is always recommended to use precious metals, such as sterling silver or gold.

Drop earrings

Headpins and eyepins are mostly used for making drop earrings and are readily available from bead stores and online suppliers.

Eyepins linked together to create dangly drop earrings.

1 Choose pins that are at least ⅓ in. (8 mm) longer than the beads that you want to thread. Run your fingers up them a few times to harden them, especially if you are using soft ones. Thread your beads, making sure that they sit neatly at the bottom. Use your wire cutters to cut off any excess length above the beads.

2 Place your pliers close to the beads and bend the wire toward you to an angle of 45 degrees. Use the hand that is holding your eyepin to hold the beads firmly in place.

3 Now take the tip of your pliers to the end of the wire and roll the wire away from you to make a neat loop above the beads. You may be able to do it in one movement, but if this isn't easy, take the pliers out of your half-made loop, reposition them, and complete the loop.

TOOLS

1 Wire cutters

2 Round-nose pliers

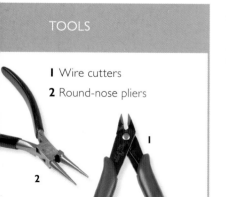

Adding an earwire

Here a fishhook earwire is shown being added to beads that are threaded onto an eyepin.

To add your earwire, place it flat onto your finger and open the loop of the earwire toward you. Place the drop that you have made into this loop and close it.

Drop earrings made with eyepins.

A bracelet made with groups of beads wired with headpins to make stems, then threaded onto a beading wire.

Other uses for headpins and eyepins

Headpins and eyepins have other uses in addition to earring making. They can be used to create a "stem" if you want to position a bead sideways. They can also be used to attach beads to a chain, either with a simple loop, as used in the drop earring opposite, or with a closed loop (see page 23).

CREATING A STEM

This enables you to use a bead in a different way and is also useful if your chosen thread is too thick for the hole in the bead.

1 Put a headpin through a bead—you can add a tiny bead to make sure that the headpin doesn't disappear into the hole. Place your round-nose pliers against the headpin and start to roll the wire.

AT-A-GLANCE SEQUENCE ▼

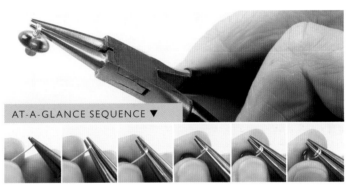

2 Keep rolling the headpin until you reach the back of your bead. To ensure that the end of the wire is close to the bead, clip off the end after rolling to make your work neat. This bead can then be threaded singly or in clusters to create an additional dimension to your work.

SIMPLE LOOPS TO HANG FROM A CHAIN

You can use your simple loops in other ways than earring making.

1 Using either headpins or eyepins, make individual drops as if you were going to make drop earrings. Use your pliers to open the top loop sideways.

2 Work this loop through a link of the chain.

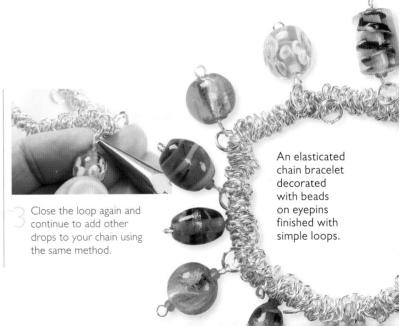

3 Close the loop again and continue to add other drops to your chain using the same method.

An elasticated chain bracelet decorated with beads on eyepins finished with simple loops.

Individual closed loops

Turquoise nuggets linked with silver wire.

These loops are one of the essentials of working with wire. They produce a secure and professional finish, and can be used to create drop earrings, pendants, and other pieces of jewelry, as shown on the following pages.

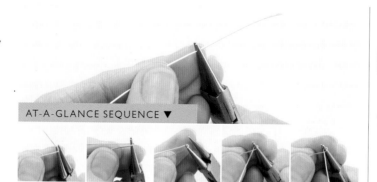

AT-A-GLANCE SEQUENCE ▼

Cut a length of wire at least 2½ in. (6 cm) longer than the length of your bead or group of beads. Practice with 22 gauge (0.6 mm) wire and a tube-shaped bead, which will be easy to handle. Grip with the round-nose pliers, about one third of the way down. Rotate them counterclockwise to create a loop, allowing for a tail of wire to close the loop.

2 Hold the loop with the chain-nose pliers and wind the tail end of the wire around the wire beneath the loop. You need to hold the wire firmly, but be careful not to let the pliers mark it or bend the loop.

TOOLS

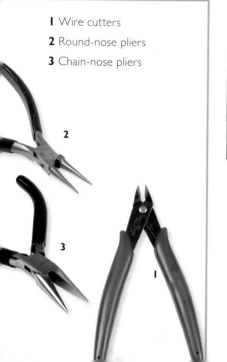

1 Wire cutters
2 Round-nose pliers
3 Chain-nose pliers

2

3

1

3 When you have wound the wire two or three times, clip the excess off neatly. Keep the flat edge of the wire cutters against the long wire as you do this.

4 Use the chain-nose pliers to gently squeeze the sharp end of the wire back beneath the coils you have just formed. You have made a closed loop to secure your beads from below. Run your fingers up the long wire a few times to strengthen and straighten it.

5 Thread on your chosen beads. It is can be easier to work with a small bead next to a closed loop. Place the round-nose pliers across the wire next to the last bead and bend the wire toward you, above the pliers.

6   Adjust the angle of the pliers to the wire, so that they are now sitting almost vertically to the beads, and use your finger and thumb to wind the wire back around the top arm of the pliers.

7   You are aiming to form another loop to match the first one, with space to wind the wire underneath the loop to close it. Stop winding when you have created the loop.

8   Holding the loop sideways with the pliers, use your other hand to wind the wire beneath the loop and back down toward the beads, to match the closed loop at the other end.

TIP   **If you want to make several similar pieces, always cut an extra piece of wire so that you can keep it as a marker for the length. Be generous with the amount of wire that you use so you don't hurt your hands.**

9   Trim off the end of the wire with the wire cutters.

10   Use the chain-nose pliers to smooth the wire back against the beads.

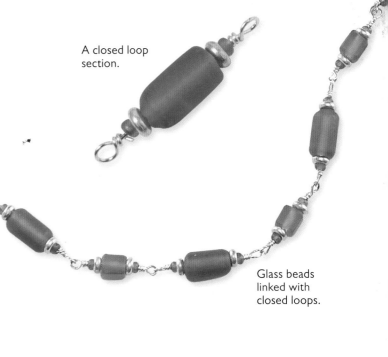

A closed loop section.

Glass beads linked with closed loops.

Closed loops with extra wire

Individual closed loop sections that have some of the wire showing can be used to make earrings or any decorative hanging pieces that you will incorporate into your designs.

When you have mastered this closed loop, you can experiment with its many different uses (see pages 21–25). The scope for design that is possible from learning this one technique is extraordinary.

1 Cut lengths of wire and make your closed loop at the bottom as on page 18. Thread your beads above this wrapped loop and decide how much wire you want to leave. Place your pliers across the wire and make a 45 degree angle. You will need to have a little over 1 in. (3 cm) left above the bend.

2 Repeat this with your other wire, if you are making earrings, so that they will be the same length.

3 Move the pliers along and roll the wire over the top nose of your pliers. Now you can wrap the wire below the loop. Cut off the end of the wire and smooth it in with the chain-nose pliers as on page 19.

Drop earrings.

Drop earrings made with closed loops that feature the wire as well as the beads.

Hanging objects

You can use closed loops with extra wire, for hanging different objects to make pendants and earrings.

FRONT-DRILLED PIECES OR DONUTS

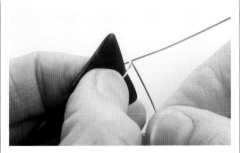

1 If your pendant has been drilled from the front, you need to take a piece of wire through the piece and fold both ends to the top.

2 Wrap the shorter end around the main wire above the pendant, leaving room for some movement. Finish this off as you would in any closed loop.

THROUGH-DRILLED PIECES

If your chosen piece is drilled through the middle, your closed loops will be the same as the basic ones, but you will need to think about the size and position of the top loop, so that you have the correct size for your chain or thong.

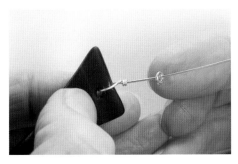

3 Add a spacer of some sort so that you can keep your ends neat. Place your pliers across the long wire and bend it toward you, leaving space for your wraps on this side.

4 Make your loop above your pendant, again thinking about the size that you need for your chain or thong. Wrap back down to your spacer bead and finish as usual.

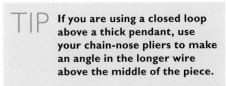

TIP **If you are using a closed loop above a thick pendant, use your chain-nose pliers to make an angle in the longer wire above the middle of the piece.**

Pendants hung in various ways, using closed loops.

Making chains with closed loops

Single beads or groups of beads can be linked together with closed loops at each end to create chains. A simple chain is shown below. As they are stiff, it can be a good idea to use a Y-shape design (see page 24) or to work with pieces of chain between the sections of beads.

TIP **Try holding your wrapping wire with your chain-nose pliers. Many people make closed loops in this way and it can be helpful when wiring lots of pieces side-by-side into a chain.**

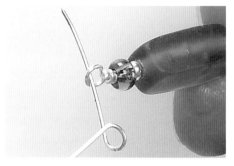

1 Start with a closed-loop section, with the loops facing in the same direction. Make the loop in the next piece of wire ready to start another section. Hook this through the top loop of your first section.

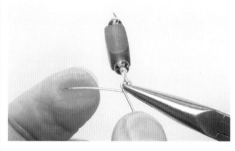

2 Wrap the bottom of the new wire as shown on page 19. Then clip off the end and neaten it with your chain-nose pliers as before.

Bracelet made with closed loops, with a ready-made fastener attached (see page 25).

3 Thread on your next section of beads.

4 Finish this top loop as shown on page 19. You can now continue with your chain of sections, varying your choice of beads if it works for your design.

Hanging pieces into a chain

To make a charm bracelet or wire into a chain for a necklace, it is more secure to attach a closed loop to the links of the chain. You can work entirely with wire, with a closed loop above and below the beads. Or you can experiment with ready-made headpins or eyepins.

A charm bracelet with a mixture of beads on headpins, beads with top- and bottom-closed loops, and little pendant pieces.

Start by making a closed loop at the bottom of a bead. Make your wrapping space above the bead, and make your loop. Work the loop through a link in your piece of chain.

When the chain is in place, hold your loop in your pliers again and wrap back down to the bead as shown on page 18. Finish off by cutting off the end of the wire and smoothing in with your chain-nose pliers. You can now add other beads or pendant pieces into the other links of the chain.

Adding ready-made chain to your design

You can work small sections of chain with suitably sized links into your closed loop chains to make them more fluid, or just to add to your range of designs.

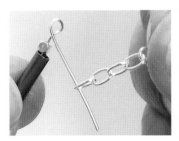

Necklace with ready-made chain.

Before you finish the top loop of your closed loop section, add a piece of chain.

Wrap below the top loop as shown on page 19.

Pick up the chain in the bottom loop of your next section and continue to build your sections, adding pieces of ready-made chain when required.

Working in a Y-shape

As closed loop chain can be a little stiff, working in a Y-shape is a good idea for necklaces.

Y-shape necklace with chain.

To work in a Y-shape, it is a good idea to work from the middle of your necklace. Make the middle drop section of the necklace first and make the top loop larger than normal. Start to make your next section of beads, dropping your first section into this larger loop.	Finish this section as before. If you are working with chain in your design, remember to add that before you close your top loop.	Now attach another wire into the first larger loop so that you can work up the other side of your necklace as well.	Work on this section in the usual way too, adding chain if necessary. Continue to build on both sides of your necklace.

Using closed loops to hang decorations

You can make more complex designs by making larger loops and hanging pieces from them.

Long crystal earrings.

First make the pieces that you want to hang. In this example long wires have been left so that the pieces will hang well together. Make a larger loop in another wire by winding around your pliers on a thicker part of the nose.	Open the loop a little so that you can put your decorative pieces into it.	You can now finish the top section as you would in all closed loop sections (see page 19).

TIP **It is good to have pliers with larger round noses to hand so that you can make larger loops. You can also wind the wire around other round objects to make loops.**

Attaching ready-made findings

You can learn to make some of your own findings to fasten your jewelry, but you are likely to also want to use ready-made fasteners. These can be attached to chains or linked sections of beads by using closed loops. This will make your work very secure.

1 You will add a little extra length when you attach a fastener, so think carefully about where you want it to be. Add another piece of wire into the last section at one end of your work. Then close this loop.

2 Add a bead to keep your ends neat.

3 Make another loop as shown on page 19 and add half of your fastener into the loop.

4 Finish wrapping below the loop. Repeat on the other side with the other half of your fastener.

TIP **Remember that if you are working with T-bar fasteners you can't have chunky beads next to the fastener. You need enough space to work it together.**

TOOLS

1 Round-nose pliers
2 Chain-nose pliers
3 Wire cutters

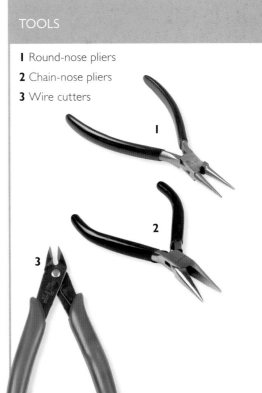

MAKING FINDINGS

The great advantage to learning to be confident with wire is that you can make many of your own findings. This will make your work very special and you will also be saved from buying lots of different types of findings for different designs.

JUMP RINGS
see page 29

Some of the findings are very basic, such as eyepins and jump rings, but it is still very satisfying to be able to make your own when necessary. How pleasing to be able to make a few spacer bars for a bracelet that you have in mind, rather than having to wait for a delivery from a supplier or having to go to the store.

For some findings, you can only make an approximation, such as headpins and T-bars. But many of the other findings can be a basis for creativity and can be great way to make your jewelry very personal. Hooks, for example, can be decorated in many different ways, allowing you to create an excellent focus for simple pieces of

DECORATED
EARWIRES
see page 32

DOUBLE-STRAND
CLASP
see page 39

DECORATIVE
COIL HOOKS
see page 41

TRIANGULAR
HOOK
see page 41

EYEPINS
see page 28

HEADPINS
see page 29

COIL EARSTUDS
see page 34

BAILS
see page 31

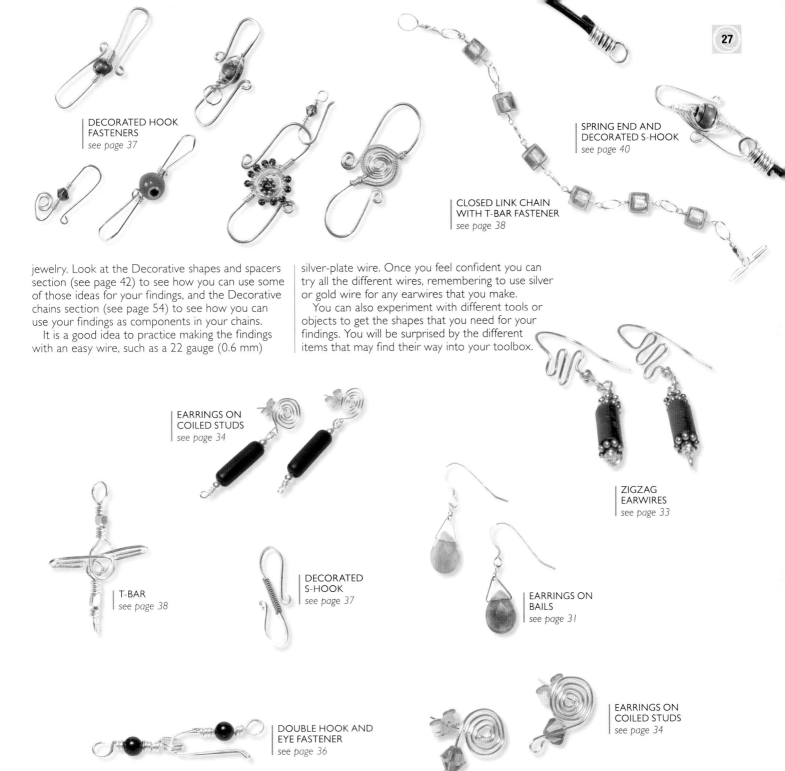

DECORATED HOOK
FASTENERS
see page 37

SPRING END AND
DECORATED S-HOOK
see page 40

CLOSED LINK CHAIN
WITH T-BAR FASTENER
see page 38

jewelry. Look at the Decorative shapes and spacers section (see page 42) to see how you can use some of those ideas for your findings, and the Decorative chains section (see page 54) to see how you can use your findings as components in your chains.

It is a good idea to practice making the findings with an easy wire, such as a 22 gauge (0.6 mm)

silver-plate wire. Once you feel confident you can try all the different wires, remembering to use silver or gold wire for any earwires that you make.

You can also experiment with different tools or objects to get the shapes that you need for your findings. You will be surprised by the different items that may find their way into your toolbox.

EARRINGS ON
COILED STUDS
see page 34

ZIGZAG
EARWIRES
see page 33

T-BAR
see page 38

DECORATED
S-HOOK
see page 37

EARRINGS ON
BAILS
see page 31

DOUBLE HOOK AND
EYE FASTENER
see page 36

EARRINGS ON
COILED STUDS
see page 34

Findings for linking

On the following pages are findings you can make that will enable you to join beads or groups of beads together.

Drop earrings made with eyepins.

Simple eyepins

You can make your own eyepins easily with most types of wire. When you have perfected this technique you are part of the way to being able to make your own earwires (see page 32). They can then be used as you would use ready-made eyepins. Remember to think of the size of the holes in your beads, when you are choosing your wire. In the Decorative Shapes and Spacers section of the book (see page 42) you can learn how to make more elaborate eyepins.

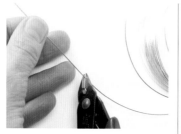

1 Simply cut two lengths of wire. You will need at least ¾ in. (2 cm) more than the length of your bead or beads. Make sure you have a good cut at the end—you can file this end for especially professional results. Bend about ⅜ in. (8 mm) of the wire toward you to an angle of 90 degrees.

2 Hold the end of your wire between the noses of your pliers and roll the wire away from you. You should be able to make a complete loop in one movement, but if this is going to put strain on your wrist, take your pliers out of the loop, and reposition them to complete the loop with a second turn.

3 Run your fingers along the eyepin a few times to harden it.

TOOLS

1 Wire cutters
2 Small file
3 Round-nose pliers
4 Hammer and block
5 Chain-nose pliers
6 Tubular objects, such as a ballpoint pen or piece of dowel (see page 30)
7 Marker pen (see page 31)

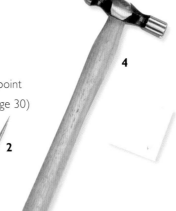

TIP **To make several eyepins with the same-sized loop, you can make a mark on your pliers to guide you. You can practice holding the wire with different parts of the noses of your pliers, to achieve different-sized loops.**

Making headpins

The headpins that you make will be rather different to ready-made ones, but this is an easy way to make very simple ones.

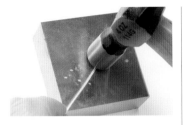

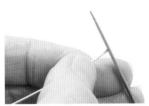

I This technique will be most successful with silver, gold, or copper wire, since if you hammer a plated wire the core color may show through. Put the end of a piece of wire onto your block and use your hammer to flatten it.

2 You can now clip off the end and file it to remove any roughness. Make sure that the bead at the bottom of the earring that you make is sufficiently tight to hold everything in place.

Drop earrings made with headpins.

Jump rings

Jump rings are a small but important part of jewelry-making. They can be used to join links in a chain, they can be half of a fastener, and they can be used in large quantities to create complex chains and chain mail as shown on pages 60–65. They can be bought ready-made in many different sizes and finishes, or you can make your own.

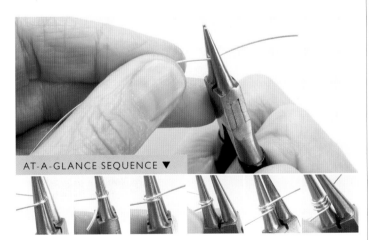

AT-A-GLANCE SEQUENCE ▼

I To make a few jump rings, hold your wire firmly between the noses of your pliers, leaving a little tail.

2 Now move your wrist counter-clockwise so that you are rolling the wire around the nose of the pliers. Hold the long end of the wire firmly in the finger and thumb of your other hand.

4 Take the loops off your pliers. Put your wire cutters into the loops, keeping them straight, between the end wires. Then cut as smoothly as you can, with one movement if possible.

3 Keep turning so that the loops build on top of each other. Keep winding until you have made the number of jump rings that you require. Stop when both the ends are on the same side.

5 Hold the rings and open them gently sideways, either with your fingers or with two pairs of pliers. File any rough edges in one direction with a small file. Make sure that the ends of the jump rings fit neatly together.

Larger jump rings

You can make different sizes by using the technique on page 29, but by winding your wire round different tubular objects, such as a ballpoint pen or piece of dowel.

1 You will press the end of your wire against the top of the pen with your finger and hold the pen from below with your thumb. Now wind the wire round the pen with your other hand, pulling as firmly as you can.

2 When you have enough loops, slide the wire off the pen and cut and finish your jump rings as on page 29.

A selection of jump rings made with various kinds of wire.

Figure-eight links

These are another useful linking component. You can use them to link parts of a chain together or try using them when you are hanging tiny pendant pieces from a chain or a beading wire, when you want your piece to hang flat.

1 Cut your wire and harden it with your fingers. Make sure you have a clean end to your wire then hold the tip between your pliers and roll away from you.

2 Now position your pliers into the angle of the loop that you have made, with the loop facing toward you.

A necklace of small silver-plate stars hanging from a beading wire with figure-eight findings.

3 Use the pliers to roll the wire in the other direction, your fingers holding it steady. Use the same part of your pliers so that your loops are the same size.

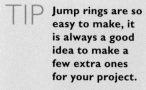

4 Now clip off the end of the wire in the middle of the figure eight. As with all other loops you will open and close them sideways when you want to use them.

TIP **Jump rings are so easy to make, it is always a good idea to make a few extra ones for your project.**

It can be a help to give the figure eights a squeeze in a pair of chain-nose pliers to flatten them.

Bails

These are not the most common findings, but they can be just what you need sometimes. They work well with pendant pieces or top-drilled beads. You need to use the thickest wire that you can fit into your chosen bead.

1 Cut a piece of wire and make a 45-degree angle with your round-nose pliers. Smooth down the wire at either side.

2 Hold the wire against the bead and make a mark where you will want it to go through the holes. If you are making a pair of earrings you could mark up a second piece of wire at the same time.

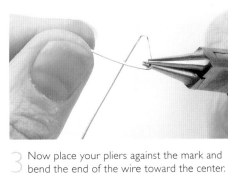

3 Now place your pliers against the mark and bend the end of the wire toward the center.

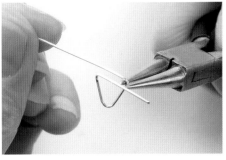

4 Copy this on the other side of the triangle.

Cherry quartz earrings made with bails and figure-eight findings.

5 Then you can cut through the center of the wires.

6 Work the ends of the bail into the hole in the bead from either side.

Earwires

You can make your own earwires and ear studs to match your designs. When you are confident with the basic shapes, there are many design possibilities.

Black agate and silver earrings on fishhook earwires.

Fishhook wires

Although you will practice your techniques with basic wires, remember to switch to pure metals when you are confident.

For each earwire you will need about 2 ½ in. (6 cm) of 20 gauge (0.8 mm) wire. File the end of the wire if it isn't very smooth. Now make a simple loop at one end, as for the eyepin on page 28.

Put your pliers above the loop to create a small space, then bend the wire to a 45-degree angle away from the open side of the loop.

Position your wire against your ballpoint pen and press your thumb into the little space that you have just made, to hold it steady. Now draw the wire round the curve of the pen so that it will keep that shape.

Now come the fun parts! Put your earwire onto a hammering block and gently hammer the back of the curve. This will strengthen the wire. It also makes it look very professional.

Cut a little off the end of the wire and gently flare it out with your round-nose pliers.

You need to get the smoothest end possible for your earwire. You can smooth the end with a cup burr or you can gently file the end. If you are using a file, work across the end first, then around the edges.

TOOLS

1 Wire cutters

2 File or cup burr

3 Round-nose pliers

4 Ballpoint pen or similar tubular object

5 Hammer and block

6 Chain-nose pliers (see page 34)

7 Ready-made scrolls to secure your earstuds (see page 34)

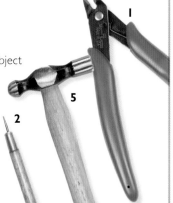

Variations

So far the earwires that you have made are very plain. There are many easy ways to decorate them to make them a little more special.

ADDING A BEAD OR CRIMP
You can make your earwires look more decorative by adding beads or French crimps.

Make the loop for your earwire as shown on page 32 and add a bead or a crimp above the loop. Place your pliers above the bead to make the next bend in the wire. Finish making your earwire as shown on page 32.

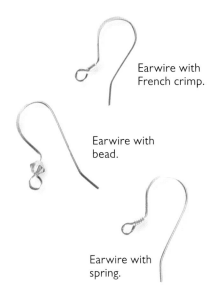

Earwire with French crimp.

Earwire with bead.

Earwire with spring.

ADDING A TINY SPRING
Adding a tiny spring or spiral of wire will make your earwires look more professional.

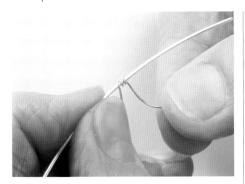

1 Make a tiny coil of wire around a piece of 20 gauge (0.8 mm) wire.

2 Slide it off and snip off and file the ends.

3 This can now be threaded onto your earwire after you have made the bottom loop and before you make the 45 degree angle. Continue to make the rest of the earwire as shown on page 32.

Earstuds

You can also make stud findings that will go through your ears. Again, remember to use pure metals when you have practiced your techniques. You will learn more about making coils in the Decorative shapes and spacers section on page 42. You may want to practice making a simple coil before you try the earstuds (see page 44).

1 Cut about 3 in. (8 cm) of 20 gauge (0.8 mm) wire for each earstud. Make a 90 degree bend in the wire about ¾ in. (2 cm) from one end. You will need to reduce this length later, but it will help you to handle the wire at this stage.

2 Place your pliers against the short wire and make a tiny circle around their tip with the longer wire, guiding the wire with your fingers.

3 Keep winding the wire, trying to make as neat a coil as you can.

4 Now hold the coil with your chain-nose pliers and continue to build it either until it stops looking neat or you have reached the size that you want.

5 Place your round-nose pliers against the end of the coil and bring the wire back around them to form a small loop below the coil. You could decorate the loop below your stud in the same way as for earwires (see page 32).

Coiled earstuds with a Venetian bead drop.

6 Clip off the end of this loop. You will open it sideways to hang a drop earring (see left).

7 Cut the straight piece of wire to the length that you like to go through your ear. Smooth the end with a file or cup burr.

Fasteners

When it comes to making fasteners for your jewelry there is a lot of scope for different designs and ideas, from simple hooks to more complex T-bar findings. You need to think carefully about which fastener will complement your design and which is the most secure.

Yellow flower turquoise stones threaded on a beading wire with a simple hook fastener.

Simple hook

The hook is very similar to an earwire (see page 32) and needs just a minor adjustment. In the bracelet shown above, it is used with a figure-eight link (see page 30). You could also hook it into a jump ring (see page 29).

> **TIP** You may want to experiment **with making your earwires in this way.**

Unless you have a very delicate piece of jewelry, you will want a fairly substantial wire for this clasp. Start with 2 in. (5 cm) of 18 gauge (1.0 mm) wire, placing the wire over a ballpoint pen, and bending down firmly on both sides. You want one end of the wire to be slightly longer than the other.

2 File the longer end to make it neat, then roll this end away with your pliers.

3 Clip the other end off so that it lines up with the middle of the loop. File this end. You may like to leave this end a little longer and roll it tightly back against the wire or use your pliers to flick out the end of the wire. Press this end in so that it is just touching the main wire.

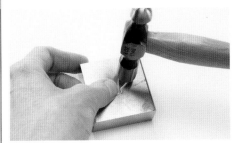

4 Finally, hammer all of the hook, unless you prefer the wire to be round, as the hammering will strengthen the hook.

TOOLS

1 Wire cutters
2 Ballpoint pen or piece of dowel
3 File
4 Round-nose pliers
5 Hammer and block
6 Chain-nose pliers (see page 36)
7 Wide-nose pliers or acrylic-nose pliers
  (see page 41)

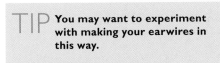

Double hook and eye

This is a more secure fastener that can either be worked into a chain that you have made or made as a separate component. It uses the same techniques as for closed loops (see page 18) and works well in either 22 gauge (0.6 mm) or 20 gauge (0.8 mm) wire.

1 For a small double hook and eye, make your first loop from 3 ½ in. (9 cm) of 22 gauge (0.6 mm) wire (see page 18). Add this to the last section of your chain if you want it to be integral.

2 Wrap the short end of the wire above this loop. Then clip off the end of the wire and smooth it back in with your chain-nose pliers.

3 Add a bead, then work out the length you want your hook to be. In this case, it extends 1 in. (2 ½ cm) above the bead. Using the tip of your pliers, double the wire back to form the top of the hook.

4 Starting at the top of the hook, run your chain-nose pliers all the way down the two wires, squeezing them together until just above the bead.

5 Now wrap the end of the wire two or three times above the bead. You will now have a length of double wire.

6 To form the hook, bend the double wire around the wider part of your pliers. Then flick up the end to complete the shape.

7 For the double eye, start on the other side in the same way. Add a bead, then place your pliers above it. Grasp the wire and bend it over the pliers at a 90 degree angle toward you.

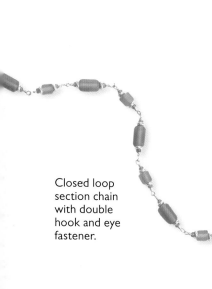

Closed loop section chain with double hook and eye fastener.

8 Move the pliers and bring your wire round the top of the pliers to start to make a loop.

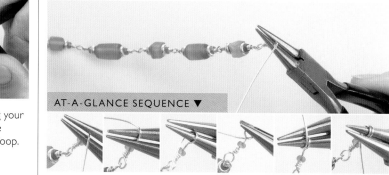

AT-A-GLANCE SEQUENCE ▼

9 The only difference between this and any other closed loop section is that you move your pliers in and out a few times so that the wire goes round twice, creating a double eye. You then finish off as before, wrapping the end of your wire down to the bead and neatening the end. Take care not to distort the double loop as you wrap beneath it.

S-hook

This is a variation on the Single hook. It is dramatic but easy to make. One of the main advantages of this hook is that you can decorate it. Once you have mastered the basic S-shape, look at the sections on Decorative shapes (see page 54) or Wrapping techniques (see page 68) and try these techniques to decorate your hooks.

Furnace bead and silver chain with a decorated S-hook.

1 Make a simple hook with 2 ¾ in. (7 cm) of 18 gauge (1.0 mm) wire. Bend one end around a ballpoint pen or larger round-nose pliers, leaving a long tail.

2 Turn your wire round and bend it the other way to make the S-shape.

3 File both ends of the wire to neaten them. Then use your round-nose pliers to make a tiny loop at each end.

4 If wished, you can hammer the hook. Push the ends together. You can use this hook with a jump ring or a figure-eight finding, or attach straight onto a large link chain.

Decorated S-hooks

Here are two of the more simple ways to decorate a hook—a wire-wrapped hook and a hook with bead.

Furnace glass and rock crystal chain with S-hook fastener.

WIRE-WRAPPED HOOK

1 This hook requires more wire: try it with a 3 in. (8 cm) length. Start exactly as before and make the first curve. Then wind a fine wire tightly around the straight end.

2 Slide the spiral of wire along the hook and make the other half of the S-shape. Trim the ends of the decorating wire.

3 With your chain-nose pliers, press the ends of the fine wire against the main wire to secure the spiral. Loop both ends as before and hammer the curves if wished.

TO DECORATE WITH A BEAD

1 Begin by making the first curve as before, allow extra wire according to the size of your bead. Then wind a length of fine 22 gauge (0.6 mm) or similar wire around the main wire as before.

2 Thread on your chosen bead and bring the thin wire to the other side of the bead.

3 Wrap the thin wire around the hook as firmly as possible. Trim the ends and slide the bead to the middle of the hook. Now make your other curve and finish as before.

T-bar

This is another very useful finding. It is especially secure for bracelets as there is no chance of it working apart. Once you have learnt the basic aspects of making it you can adapt it for your designs.

1. Start by making the T of the T-bar. You will need 2 ¾ in. (7 cm) of 20 gauge (0.8 mm) wire. Smooth the wire, then bend it around your round-nose pliers to form a loop in the center.

2. Check the measurements on either side of the loop to check that it is central and trim off any excess wire. Use your round-nose pliers to fold the end of the wire over on one side— you will need to fold over about ¼ in. (7 mm). Use your chain-nose pliers to squeeze both sides of the folded wire together.

3. Now fold again so that you create as neat a bar as you can. Then repeat on the other side.

4. Cut about 2 ¾ in. (7 cm) of wire for the stem. This is a simple closed loop section as shown on page 18. Make a loop at one end (this can be linked into the last section of a chain that you are working on). Add a small bead above the wraps. Make the top loop in the normal way, then drop the T-bar that you have made into this. Wrap back down to the bead as before.

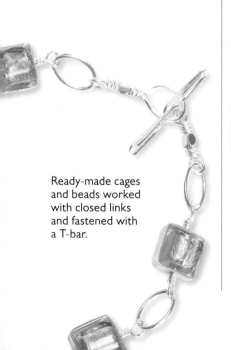

Ready-made cages and beads worked with closed links and fastened with a T-bar.

5. The circle that your T-bar will go into is also made as a closed loop section. Start with 3 ½ in. (9 cm) of wire and make a wrapped loop, remembering to add it onto a chain if necessary. Add a bead, then place your pliers above it to allow space along the wire for wrapping.

6. Make the circle above this space at 90 degrees to the first loop. Either form it around an object such as a pen, or use a pair of round-nose pliers with larger noses.

7. When you have made the circle, wrap the end of the wire back down to the bead and finish off as usual.

Double-strand clasp

Double-drilled pearl bracelet.

Some designs have two rows of chain or are double-threaded. To fasten them, you can bring both strands into one clasp, or you can use this simple double clasp.

1 Cut 3 ½ in. (9 cm) of 20 gauge (0.8 mm) wire for the hook. Place your round-nose pliers in the center of the wire and double it over. Use your chain-nose pliers to squeeze the wires together.

2 Roll the double wire over your round-nose pliers to create a hook.

3 Below the hook, bend the two ends of the wire to an angle of 90 degrees against the hook.

4 Make sure that the remaining pieces of wire are the same length. Trim off any excess wire. Using your pliers as shown, roll each end of the wire to make a loop. Flick up the end of the hook a little.

5 For the eye, you will need about 2 ⅜ in. (6 cm) of the same wire. Holding the wire in the center with your pliers, make a U-shape.

6 Flick out the wire on either side of this shape.

7 Trim off the ends and roll a loop in each end to match the hook.

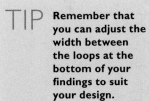

TIP **Remember that you can adjust the width between the loops at the bottom of your findings to suit your design.**

Spring end

This is another small finding that you can make yourself. It is designed to be used with leather or cotton thonging. You will need to add a hook or a ready-made fastener to link the two sides together.

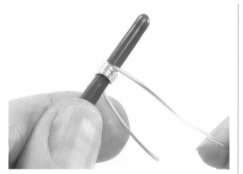

Use 20 gauge (0.8 mm) wire as on the previous pages. You can work with the wire straight off your reel, rather than cutting short lengths. Wind it around a smooth, tubular object such as the handle of a file, or a pen. You will need to make six or seven circles of wire, wound as close to each other as possible.

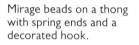

When you have removed the little spiral of wire from its support and cut off the ends, slide your round-nose pliers under the top loop to lift it a little.

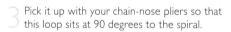

Mirage beads on a thong with spring ends and a decorated hook.

Two spring ends connected with a decorated hook.

3 Pick it up with your chain-nose pliers so that this loop sits at 90 degrees to the spiral.

4 Neaten the loop at the other end of the spiral. Your thong will be pushed into these spring ends and the last loop will be pressed into the thong to hold the spring end in place.

Coil hook

If you look at the section on Decorative shapes (see page 42) there are many examples of designs that you can adapt to turn into fasteners or earwires. This coil is a good one to try first as it will look very dramatic when you incorporate it into its designs. Before you make the hook, you may want to refer to page 44, which explains how to make a coil.

Picasso jasper necklace with triangular hook.

1 Try making a coil hook with about 9 in. (21 cm) of 18 gauge (1.0 mm) wire. Make sure you have a good cut at one end, filing it if necessary. Roll up this end with your round-nose pliers.

2 Use your wide-nose or acrylic-nose pliers and make a coil (see page 44), stopping just before your chosen size.

3 Hold the wire just below the coil with your pliers and bend the wire gently away from the coil.

4 Insert the pliers into the angle you have made in the wire and curve the wire around them so that you make a U-shape against the coil.

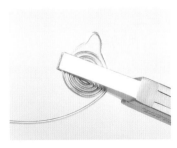

5 Continue to form the coil. Finish working it when you are opposite the U-shape.

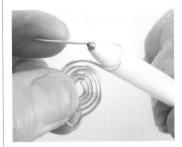

6 Place the widest part of your round-nose pliers, or a rounded object such as a pen, against the edge of the coil and draw the wire back in the other direction, to form a hook.

7 Trim any excess wire, file the end, and roll over the tip of the wire. You can use a jump ring or just link this hook into a loop at the other side.

Metallic bead bracelet with coil hook.

TIP **This hook can be decorated with spirals or wire, or by hammering it. You could use the same technique to make a hook in a triangular or square shape.**

DECORATIVE SHAPES AND SPACERS

One of the main advantages of working with wire is the ability to create a range of different shapes to make your jewelry individual. The possibilities are huge—the same shape made with a different gauge or type of wire will look very different.

It makes a lot of sense to practice making each shape in different types of wire to see how it affects the result. For example, a star shape will work well in a silver-plated wire, which is a crisp wire, whereas the same shape will tend to look more rounded made in a copper wire.

Colored wires produce wonderfully vibrant results, but need to be handled with extra care, since they mark easily. Some shapes respond well to being hammered. This strengthens the wire and alters the shape. However, if you hammer a shape that has crossed wires you will destroy the wire.

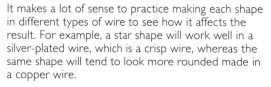
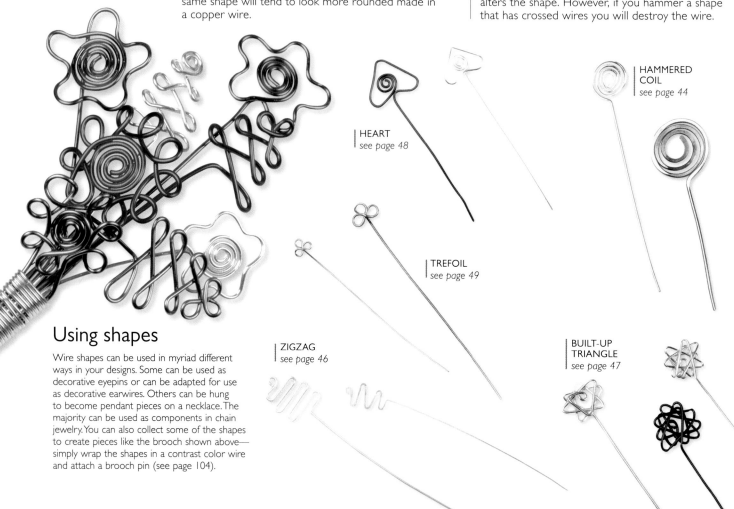

HAMMERED
COIL
see page 44

HEART
see page 48

TREFOIL
see page 49

ZIGZAG
see page 46

BUILT-UP
TRIANGLE
see page 47

Using shapes

Wire shapes can be used in myriad different ways in your designs. Some can be used as decorative eyepins or can be adapted for use as decorative earwires. Others can be hung to become pendant pieces on a necklace. The majority can be used as components in chain jewelry. You can also collect some of the shapes to create pieces like the brooch shown above— simply wrap the shapes in a contrast color wire and attach a brooch pin (see page 104).

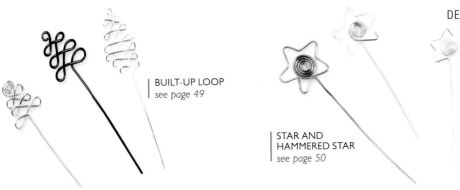

BUILT-UP LOOP
see page 49

STAR AND
HAMMERED STAR
see page 50

FLOWER
WITH PETALS
see page 50

You will learn more about different wires as you practice making different shapes and you can also learn a lot about the benefits of different tools. You can try making the same shape with small, neat round-nose pliers or with a heavier pair and assess your results. If you are going to work with a lot of colored wires, it is worth trying some pliers with acrylic noses that won't mark the wire so much. You can also try hammering on different surfaces, but a small hammering block is a good investment.

SPACER BARS
see page 51

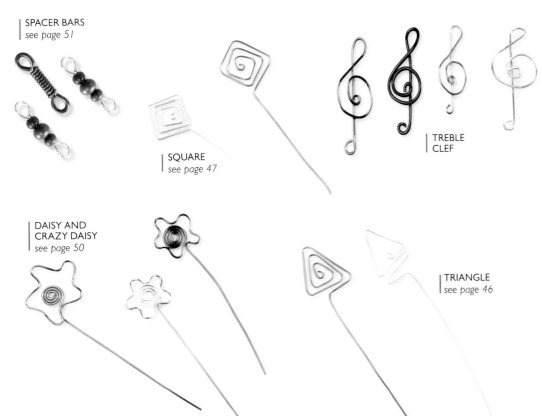

SQUARE
see page 47

TREBLE
CLEF

DAISY AND
CRAZY DAISY
see page 50

TRIANGLE
see page 46

EARRINGS CREATED
WITH A JIG
see page 53

Making shapes

On the following pages are some of the shapes that you can try making in many different wires.

Simple coils of colored, plain, and hammered wire threaded on beading wire.

Coils

The coil is such a useful shape that in many books it is considered a core technique. It is important to learn to make it, but there also specialized tools for making coils that you may like to try out at a later stage. A coil can be used in many different ways and there are several ways in which you can make one. As always, experiment with different wires and try hammering the end result to see what effect you can produce.

TIP **Pliers with acrylic noses would be useful for holding the coil as you are working so that you don't mark the wire, especially in the case of colored wire.**

TOOLS

1 Wire cutters
2 Chain-nose pliers
3 Hammer and block (optional)
4 Round-nose pliers (see page 46)
5 Wide-nose pliers (see page 49)

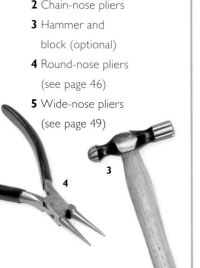

AT-A-GLANCE SEQUENCE ▼

3 Open the chain-nose pliers to move the coil so that you can continue to build it.

SIMPLE COIL

1 To make your first coil, start with 4 in. (10 cm) of 22 gauge (0.6 mm) wire. Make a tiny loop in the end of the wire with the tip of your pliers. The neater this is, the better your coil will be.

2 Holding the loop with your chain-nose pliers, use your fingers to draw the rest of the wire around the loop to start building the coil.

4 Stop when you are near the end of the wire, or when the coil has started to lose its shape. You can vary the finished coil by straightening the remaining wire to make an eyepin. For a decorative shape, hold the coil between your fingers and use your pliers to roll the remaining wire into a small loop on which to hang the shape. If preferred, you can turn the loop sideways so that the shape hangs differently.

Linked bracelet with coil decorations and glass beads.

WIND-BACK COIL

Experiment with this variation. It is especially useful if you want to make coils that go in two different directions, or if you are finishing a piece of wire with a coil. This method requires you to use your hand rather like a pair of pliers to hold the coil, so you may find it tiring.

1 Cut 4 in. (10 cm) of 22 gauge (0.6 mm) wire. Mark the center of the wire and make your first coil as on page 44. Now make a small loop at the other end of the wire, facing in the opposite direction.

2 Hold the loop firmly in your chain-nose pliers and, holding the coiled end with your hand to keep it still and steady, wind back down the wire with the pliers to create a second coil.

3 Keep winding until the coils are positioned as you want them.

DOUBLE COIL

You can use a coil as a spacer, but you need to make it in a different way. This type of coil is a useful component that you can attach at both sides.

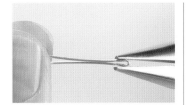

1 Cut a longer piece of 22 gauge (0.6 mm) wire— say, 6 in. (15 cm) long. Place your round-nose pliers in the center of the wire and bend the wire in half. Press both sides together with your chain-nose pliers.

2 Now the tricky bit—hold the folded end with your chain-nose pliers and gently start to roll this end. Hold the remaining wire in place with your hand. Use all the strength in your arm, not just your wrist.

3 Continue to form the double coil until it starts to lose its shape, or you reach the size that you need.

4 Now bend the first of the wires away from the coil.

5 Continue to coil the other wire until you reach the other side of the coil and bend this away too. You can add beads to either side of the coil, or use it as a link in a chain of beads. You can hammer it to strengthen it.

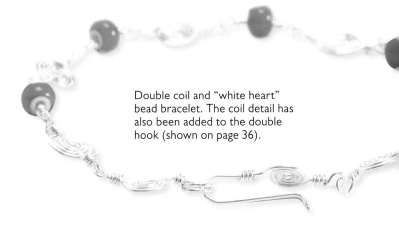

Double coil and "white heart" bead bracelet. The coil detail has also been added to the double hook (shown on page 36).

Zigzag

A zigzag is really fun to make. It is easiest as a fairly random shape within a design. If you want to make zigzags that are very regular you could explore the use of a jig, as shown on page 53.

1 Using 3 ½ in. (9 cm) of 20 gauge (0.8 mm) wire, roll a small loop at one end. Place your pliers at different points along the wire and bend it around them, making your zigzag as neat or as crazy as you like. Try using different parts of your pliers to get tighter or rounder shapes.

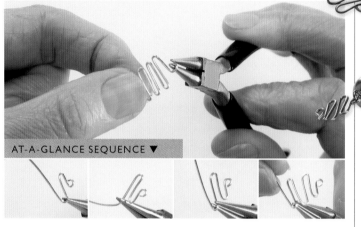

AT-A-GLANCE SEQUENCE ▼

2 Roll another loop at the end of your zigzag. You will need about ⅜ in. (1 cm) to roll the loop.

Zigzag necklace with single loops and spring ends to attach the thong.

Triangle drop earrings.

Triangle

This is a shape that works well for eyepins or for decorations that you can hang from chains. As with other shapes, the skill lies in making the subsequent shapes to match.

TIP **To create a matching pair, try working on two wires at the same time for each step.**

1 For an eyepin with a generous stem, cut 3 ½ in. (9 cm) of 22 gauge (0.6 mm) or 20 gauge (0.8 mm) wire. Start with a tiny loop at one end. Then hold the loop with your pliers and straighten the wire next to it.

2 Holding the wire with your pliers, continue to straighten with your fingers, drawing it out at a 45-degree angle.

3 Move your pliers down to what will be the bottom of the triangle and make another 45-degree bend.

4 Your final angle will need to be made slightly higher than the first one so that the wire can run above the first loop. Finish off by making a right angle in this wire—your eyepin is ready to be used.

Chain bracelet with built up triangles and crystals and a T-bar fastener.

Built-up triangle

This shape can also be used for eyepins and decorations. It is easier to make with finer-gauge wires.

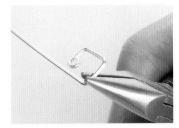

1 Try making this triangle, using 4 ¾ in. (12 cm) of 22 gauge (0.6 mm) wire. Start by making a tiny loop in the wire, as for the regular triangle on page 46. Make the first two angles as before. Then make the next angle sharper so that your wire crosses over into the middle of the first side.

2 Aim the next angle toward the middle of the opposite side.

3 Your next turn will take the wire back toward the loop.

4 You have been working from the back of the shape. Continue in this way until you are happy with the shape that you have created when you turn it over. Make a right angle in the remaining wire to create the stem for your eyepin, or a loop for a decoration.

Square

This shape is very similar to the triangle and can be used in many of the same ways. You can vary the amount of times that you bend your wire around the square.

1 For a square to use as an eyepin, cut 4 in. (10 cm) of 22 gauge (0.6 mm) or 20 gauge (0.8 mm) wire. Make a small loop at one end with your round-nose pliers. Then, with either your chain-nose or round-nose pliers, make a right angle in the wire just along from the loop, to start the square. Continue to form the square by making a second and third corner.

2 Make a fourth corner in the wire to take it just above your loop. Continue creating the square shape, taking the wire around the corners as many times as you like.

3 When you have finished building your shape, bend the end of the wire back at a right angle to create an eyepin.

Heart

This is a great shape to use for romantic jewelry. The heart shape is perfect for making decorations to hang on a necklace or bracelet, or it can become an excellent eyepin.

Hammered heart pendant with an amethyst bead.

1 Experiment with 4 in. (10 cm) of 22 gauge (0.6 mm) or 20 gauge (0.8 mm) wire. Start with a small coil, as shown on page 44. Bend the wire around your round-nose pliers so that it takes the curve of the pliers.

2 Move your pliers down the wire and bend the wire below the coil as shown.

3 Now place your pliers against the wire at the same height as your first curve and make a second curve, drawing the wire down behind the coil.

4 Finally, place your chain-nose pliers against the wire just above the coil and make a tight turn so that it creates a stem for your heart.

Linking square

By making a simple variation on the square (see page 47) you can create a square that you can use as a spacer or in a chain.

TIP **You can hammer the linking square, but be very careful where the wires cross so that you don't sheer them.**

1 Start this shape in exactly the same way as the square on page 47, but allow an extra ¾–1 in. (2–3 cm) of wire. Stop when you get to the side that will be third from the end. Coil the wire counterclockwise against your round-nose pliers to create a loop in the middle of this side. Wind the loop with your pliers and make it as central as possible.

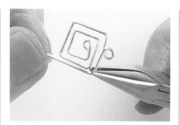

2 When you have made this loop, continue making the angles in the wire until you reach the opposite side of the square.

3 Cut the wire on the final side so that it overlaps the square a little bit. Now roll this back with your round-nose pliers to create another loop on this side.

Earrings with squares and linking squares.

Trefoil

This is another series of shapes that are based on building up small loops of wire. The trefoil shape makes pretty eyepins. However, it can't be easily hammered as the wires cross.

Trefoil eyepins linked to create earrings.

1 Using 3 ½ in. (9 cm) of 22 gauge (0.6 mm) wire, make a small loop with your round-nose pliers. Turn the wire over and make a matching loop opposite to create a figure-of-eight shape.

2 Draw the wire on past the second loop and make a third loop beneath it.

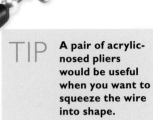

3 When the third loop is complete, give the shape a little squeeze with your wide-nose pliers, then flick the long wire back to center it against the trefoil.

TIP

A pair of acrylic-nosed pliers would be useful when you want to squeeze the wire into shape.

You can try setting beads into the built-up loop as you build it.

Built-up loops

This is a shape that can be made easily by hand. It can be used for elaborate eyepins or for spacers. If you are using it as a spacer, you may want to try making it with a jig (see page 53). Building it by hand creates more delicate pieces, but a jig will give you greater uniformity.

1 Try this with 5 in. (13 cm) of 22 gauge (0.6 mm) wire. (You will need more wire if you want to make a very elaborate eyepin.) Make a small loop at the end of the wire with your round-nose pliers. Then move the pliers a little way along the wire and make another loop, under the wire and facing toward the first loop. Keep hardening the wire with your fingers as you work.

2 Turn the piece over and, on the other side of your first loop, form another loop like your second one. Gently flatten the shape with your chain-nose pliers as you work.

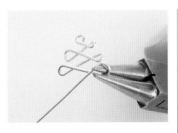

3 Continue in this way, working from side to side building up the shape to your design. You can make the shape wider and wider, or create more of a diamond. Experiment with how you use your pliers to make tighter or rounder loops. To finish, you can either make another central loop to form a spacer, or turn up a straight wire to create an eyepin.

Pearl and wire earrings with built-up loop spacer.

Daisy

The daisy is another fairly easy shape to build. You can make it very precise or you can allow it to be more freeform. Once you have mastered it in a plain wire, it is a great shape to try in colored wires.

1 For your first daisy, try using 5 in. (13 cm) of 22 gauge (0.6 mm) wire. Start with a coil, then run your fingers up the remaining wire to curve it away from the coil. Gripping the wire next to the coil with your round-nose pliers, make a U-shaped loop round them—this is the first petal.

2 Place your pliers next to the petal and bend the wire into an angle against the coil. Insert the pliers into this angle and make a second U-shaped petal. Continue making petals around the coil. You may need to practice so that the petals fit around the coil neatly.

3 When you have completed your petals, hold the remaining wire with the pliers and draw it away from the daisy to create a stem.

TIP

You can work this shape in a similar way but more loosely to create an abstract flower or "splash" shape.

To create a star shape, try bending the petals into V-shapes instead of U-shapes.

Crazy daisy earrings.

Flower with petals

This is a different way to create a flower shape that is fun to make. As it has separated loops, you could try using it as a spacer as well.

1 You will need quite a lot of wire for this shape. Start with 6 in. (15 cm) of 22 gauge (0.6 mm) wire. Begin by making a coil. Place your round-nose pliers against the coil and roll the wire back against itself to create a loop—the first petal. You will need to reposition the pliers a little as you make the loop to widen it.

2 Draw the wire on past the first loop, leaving space for the next one, then roll the wire back into this space to make the next petal. Continue working around the coil, building the petals as you go. The difficult part of the process is making the right number of same-size petals to fit around the coil.

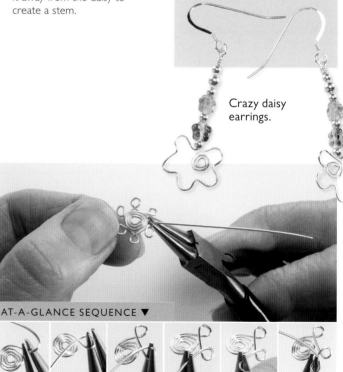

AT-A-GLANCE SEQUENCE ▼

3 Squeeze the piece into shape with your chain-nose pliers. You can finish by drawing the long wire up to create an eyepin, or you can cut the wire off close to the last loop to create a spacer.

More spacers

There are other spacers that you may consider making, mainly by using loops in different ways or adapting the shapes that you have learnt.

Open coil

The double coil, which makes an excellent spacer, has been explained (see page 45), but you can also make an open coil as a linking piece. The only difference between this and the basic coil shown earlier is that this coil starts with a larger loop.

1 Begin by making a loop, remembering that it must be larger than in the basic coil. Either use larger pliers, or work further up the nose of your small pliers.

2 Holding the loop in your wide-nose pliers, build the coil as for the one on page 45. To finish, make it an eyepin or trim off all the excess wire to create a decorative circle.

Open coil earrings with small Czech Republic beads.

Spacer bars and hangers

There are lots of ways to use loops to extend your designs. They are mostly simple ideas but the skill lies in making them as precise as possible. You may want to consider using a marker pen to mark the wire or your pliers to help create uniformity.

DUMBBELL SPACER BAR
Made up of two simple loops with a space between them, this is very similar to the figure-eight link finding on page 30.

1 For this simple version of the spacer, start with 1 in. (2.5 cm) of 20 gauge (0.8 mm) wire. Make a simple loop on one side.

2 Now turn the wire over and make a second loop of the same size on the other side of the wire.

TIP **Try making the spacer bar above in lots of different ways: you can use a bead between the loops; face the loops in the same direction; wire-wrap the space between them; or hammer them.**

Spacer bars with mirage beads on memory wire.

TOOLS

1 Round-nose pliers
2 Wide-nose pliers
3 Chain-nose pliers
4 Wire cutters
5 Hammer and block
  (optional)

TRIPLE SPACER BARS

You can extend the double spacer by adding an extra loop at the center. Then you can work three strands into it.

1 Allow an extra ⅜ in. (1 cm) of wire and make a loop in the center of it by rolling it around your round-nose pliers.

2 Then you can roll in the ends of the wire to complete the spacer bar.

Triple spacer bar earring with miracle beads.

Looped spacer bars or hangers

This design or variations on it can be used to create hangers for elaborate earrings or end bars for multiple-strand necklaces or bracelets.

DOUBLE HANGER

Start with a simple shape. This is very similar to the triple spacer.

1 Try this with 2 in. (5 cm) of 20 gauge (0.8 mm) wire. Make a loop in the center of the wire.

2 Now roll in the ends of the wire to make loops on either side.

MULTIPLE HANGER

This is a slightly more complicated version.

1 A 3 in. (18 cm) length of 20 gauge (0.8mm) wire works well for this shape. Start with the central loop as before. Then make loops on either side by placing your round-nose pliers against the wire, pulling the wire around them, and rolling with your pliers at the same time.

2 Now you can roll in the ends of the wire to complete the shape.

Star and dangling star multiple earrings.

TIP If you are making a lot of matching pieces you may want to mark the nose of your pliers so that you make the same size of loop.

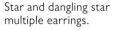

Using a jig

As well as making spacers and hangers freehand, you can also create them using a jig. Jigs are like small pegboards that allow you to create patterns with wire that you can incorporate into your designs.

Button necklace with 'jig' spacers.

TIP **This is just one of many possible designs. You can follow published designs, copy the design shown on this page, or create your own.**

How to use a jig

The advantage of using a jig is that you can recreate complex shapes many times so that each piece you make will be very similar. If you invest in one, you can also use it to make earwires. Most jigs now come with a spiral maker, which makes coils.

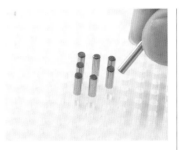

1 For these complex zigzag pieces you will need 8 in. (20 cm) of 20 gauge (0.8 mm) wire. Set up the pegs on the board—for this shape create a tight square with a hole in the middle.

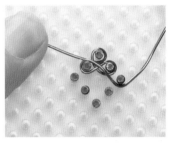

2 Start off by winding the wire counterclockwise around the top peg, ensuring that there is enough spare wire at the end to give you a good hold.

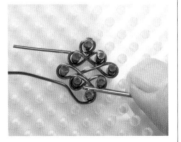...

3 Work your way round the rest of the pegs. For this design, cross from right to left, going counterclockwise around the right-hand pegs and clockwise around the left-hand pegs. To create a tight shape, pull firmly as you work so that the wire is firmly wound.

TOOLS

1 Jig

2 Wire cutters

3 Acrylic-nosed pliers

4 Large darning needle or similar (see Step 4)

4 Press the wire down between the pegs with the darning needle.

5 When you have completed the shape, cut off the excess wire from the top and bottom loop. To harden the wire you can press the shape with a pair of acrylic-nosed pliers.

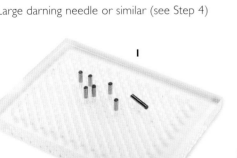

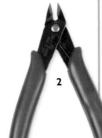

DECORATIVE CHAINS

This section builds upon the techniques covered in the previous ones. As with the other techniques that have been covered, the emphasis is on practicing the techniques over and over. As you are working, think about how you could link all the techniques you have learned together to create new designs.

The basics of simple chains have already been covered. The most simple way of making a chain would be to link together a series of the jump rings covered on page 29. This can then be extended to create the complex linked chains also known as chain mail, which are shown on pages 62–65.

You can try linking together other combinations of the shapes that you have learned. Examples have been given to inspire your chain making. Look at the Gallery section of the book (see pages 136–155) to see how exciting chains can become.

The great enjoyment of making chains is that you can make your component pieces then build your designs as you work. Remember to start by practicing with inexpensive wires, and once you are confident you can transfer your skills to working with precious wires.

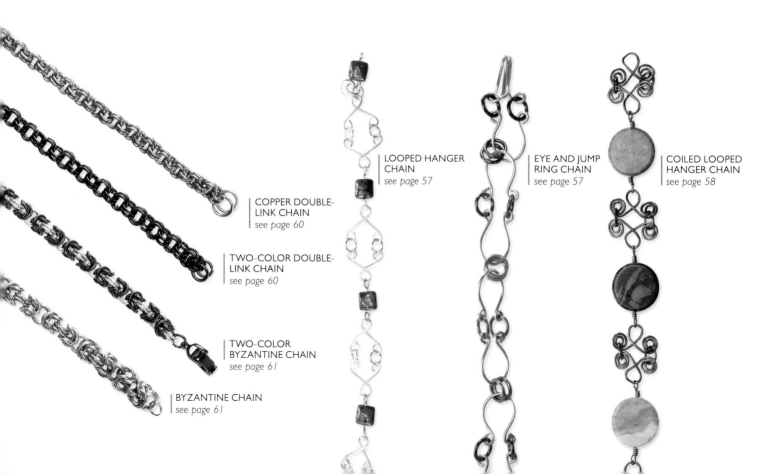

LOOPED HANGER
CHAIN
see page 57

EYE AND JUMP
RING CHAIN
see page 57

COILED LOOPED
HANGER CHAIN
see page 58

COPPER DOUBLE-
LINK CHAIN
see page 60

TWO-COLOR DOUBLE-
LINK CHAIN
see page 60

TWO-COLOR
BYZANTINE CHAIN
see page 61

BYZANTINE CHAIN
see page 61

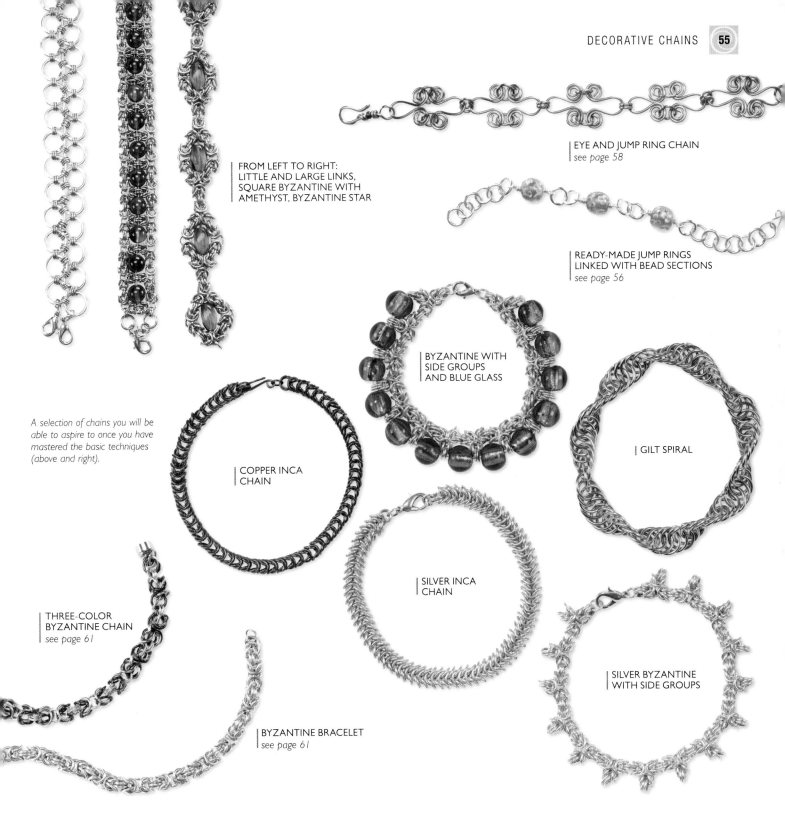

FROM LEFT TO RIGHT:
LITTLE AND LARGE LINKS,
SQUARE BYZANTINE WITH
AMETHYST, BYZANTINE STAR

EYE AND JUMP RING CHAIN
see page 58

READY-MADE JUMP RINGS
LINKED WITH BEAD SECTIONS
see page 56

BYZANTINE WITH
SIDE GROUPS
AND BLUE GLASS

A selection of chains you will be
able to aspire to once you have
mastered the basic techniques
(above and right).

COPPER INCA
CHAIN

GILT SPIRAL

SILVER INCA
CHAIN

THREE-COLOR
BYZANTINE CHAIN
see page 61

SILVER BYZANTINE
WITH SIDE GROUPS

BYZANTINE BRACELET
see page 61

Simple decorative chains

On the following pages are some initial design ideas for decorative chains. Use your imagination to come up with more designs.

Furnace slices and wire S-hook and jump-ring chain.

S-hook and jump-ring chain

Once you know how to make S-hooks and jump rings, it's an easy task to link them together to make this chain.

1 Following the instructions on page 37, make some S-hooks with 2 ½ in. (6 cm) lengths of 20 gauge (0.8 mm). Use the same gauge of wire to make some jump rings, as shown on page 29. Hammer them if you like this look. Hammering will also work harden the links.

2 Open your jump rings sideways, as described on page 29, drop in your S-hooks, then close them as shown.

3 Continue to build your chain in this way, adding beads if you wish to make it more decorative. Squeeze your S-hooks together after linking to the jump rings so there are no gaps for the rings to slide through.

TOOLS

1 Wire cutters

2 Ballpoint pen or doweling

3 Small file

4 Round-nose pliers

5 Hammer and block (optional)

6 Wide-nose or chain-nose pliers

TIP **You can use the same hook and jump ring as a fastener or opt for another style to differentiate.**

Remember that you can replace the jump rings with beads or sections of beads on wire.

Eye and jump-ring chain

This is another chain that you will have learnt to make without knowing it, if you have worked through earlier pages. You will need to make a few adjustments and link your components. This chain can also be hammered.

1 For this chain you will need to make a wider eye than the one on page 56, so it's best to wind it around a ballpoint pen. The eye here uses 1 ½ in. (4 cm) of 20 gauge (0.8 mm) wire. Pull the wire around the pen to make the main curve for your link.

2 Trim off any excess wire so that the sides are even, then roll them up toward the curved top of the eye. Next make your jump rings, ensuring that you have enough to allow you to keep building your chain.

3 Link your chain with two jump rings between the curves of the eyes and one between each of the small loops on the eyes, as shown in the finished bracelet on the right.

Bracelet made from 16 gauge (1.3 mm) tinned copper wire and ready-made jump rings.

Looped hanger chain

This is yet another chain that has been demonstrated on previous pages. The hanger finding is shown on page 52 and is again looped with jump rings.

Silver and pyrite looped hanger bracelet.

1 Make a number of hanger findings as shown on page 52. The example here, which makes quite a delicate chain, uses 1 ½ in. (4 cm) of 20 gauge (0.8 mm) wire. Also make plenty of jump rings to link the pieces. If you hammer these components, take care at the points where the wires cross so that you don't damage them.

2 Link your pieces with one or two jump rings between the central loop. Then use single jump rings between the side loops.

Coil chains

There are lots of different ways to make use of the coiling technique explained on page 44. You can extend both the eye and jump ring and looped hanger chains on page 59 simply by adding coils to them.

Coiled eye and jump-ring chain.

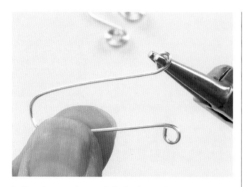

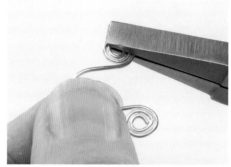

For the sections of chain shown here, you will need 3 ½ in. (9 cm) of 20 gauge (0.8 mm) wire. Start by curving the middle of the wire around the pen or your round-nose pliers to make an eye as on page 59. Now make a generous loop at each end of the wire. It is better to work on both sides at once so that you can make them match.

2 Using your chain-nose or wide-nose pliers, coil each side back up the wire toward the center until you achieve a shape that you like. Now make the jump rings to go with these links. Remember that they will have to be large to fit through the coiled ends.

3 Build the chain with your jump rings. Put one or two between the curves of the eyes and work single jump rings through the coils.

Coiled looped hanger chain with Picasso jasper discs.

LOOPED HANGER CHAIN
This is made in exactly the same way but with the crossed-over loop shown on page 52 instead of the curved top.

Coil links chain

There are many other ways of using coils as chains. Here is another example that you might like to try.

Silver coil and Dalmatian jasper coil chain.

1 For this chain, you will need 3 in. (8 cm) of 20 gauge (0.8 mm) wire. If you make it without a bead or with a smaller bead you will need less. Start by forming a loop in the end of the wire. Make it quite wide so that another wire can go through it later. Now build your coil, as on page 44. Bend back the wire at a 90-degree angle to the coil. Make the next coil in the same way.

2 Add a bead if you wish, then bend the wire toward you with your round-nose pliers.

3 Using your larger round-nose pliers again, roll the wire away to make a large loop.

4 Open this loop sideways and slide the next piece that you have made into it. Close the loop again. Continue to build the chain.

TIP **With all of these designs you will find that it helps to experiment with larger and smaller pliers, changing them for different actions. Acrylic-nosed pliers will be very helpful for making the coils.**

Linked jump-ring chains

Double or two-link chain.

Chains of different complexities can be made with jump rings, from a basic chain to the more complex tubular pieces made with the chain-mail technique.

Double or two-link chain

The double or two-link chain is one of the basic chain designs and is an excellent one to try first.

1 In this example, 4 mm jump rings made with 14 gauge (1.6 mm) wire are used, in two different colors to show how the chain builds. Open a jump ring by twisting it sideways (see page 15).

2 Now hang two closed rings into this ring.

3 Twist the ring closed using your two pairs of pliers. Make sure your ring has closed neatly.

4 Open another ring and pass it through the two rings that you added in the last step. Twist it closed, as before, letting the other rings hang down while you do so. This ring will become the pair to the ring that you first started with.

TOOLS

▪ Any two pairs of chain-nose pliers (mini and long used in this section)

5 Now hold the rings so that you have two pairs of rings looped into each other. Add your fifth ring through both of the rings in one of the pairs. If you are using different colors you will need to alternate them.

6 Add another ring through the same pair, allowing the last one to drop to one side as you do so. You will keep building your chain by adding more rings in this same way until the chain is your required length.

7 To add your clasp, it is usually easiest to put a ring through the last pair of rings and through the catch, then close it, rather than trying to put the catch directly onto a pair of rings.

Byzantine chain

The Byzantine chain is a little more complex but is a very good progression from the double-link chain opposite. It is a good idea to practice by using different colored jump rings before you embark on a necklace or bracelet.

Byzantine chain.

1 In this example, 4 mm jump rings made of 16 gauge (1.25 mm) wire are used, in four colors to help you to see where the links go. You will need a larger ring to start your chain. Link the first pair of rings side by side into this large ring.

2 Add a second pair through both of the first two rings (red) and then add another pair into this second pair (black). This is the same as starting a double chain.

3 Fold the third pair of rings (black) back so that they lie over the first pair (blue), then separate the second pair (red) so that there is a space between them. This makes the first "knot" section.

4 Now link two more rings into the third pair (black) between the second pair (red). This is a joining pair, which will be seen between the knots.

5 Now add two more pairs, in the same colors as your third (black) and second (red) pairs, working as you did before in the double chain.

6 Fold the last pair that you added back over the previous pair to make a second "knot" in the opposite direction to the first one.

7 Separate the rings of the last knot so that you can add the next joining pair to the last pair that you added. This will sit between the rings of the previous pair, and is the same color as the first pair of rings that you used (blue). Note that this joining pair is at right angles to the previous joining pair—the directions will alternate along the chain.

8 Add two more pairs of rings in the double chain manner as in Step 2, and continue to work in this way until your chain is as long as you need it. Try to end with a second "knot" finished to make your design symmetrical. At the end, add a single ring in place of the usual linking pair, and attach your clasp onto it before closing this ring. The original larger ring can be used to connect the clasp at the other end, or it can be replaced with another suitable single ring.

 TIP **Instead of using a larger ring at the start of the chain, you may find a piece of scrap wire, that is twisted together, easier to hold.**

When working on these chains, experiment with different pliers and see what sort you prefer. Some people are comfortable with mini pliers, others prefer bent-nosed pliers—with practice, you will discover what feels comfortable to you.

Flat chain mail

This technique is also known as chain mail. It is a great way to create flat sections of linked rings for bracelets or pendants.

1 In this example, 4 mm jump rings made from 18 gauge (1 mm) wire have been used, with an elaborate clasp with four loops that will hold the first row of jump rings. Start by opening a jump ring and hang one of the loops of one end of the catch and a second jump ring onto it. Then close the ring and repeat all along the row of loops. If you do not have a suitable clasp, hang the four sets of rings on to a scrap of wire that can be removed later.

2 Lie your piece so that the four rings in the second row lie flat on the work surface next to each other.

3 Now add a jump ring to connect the first two rings. It will go through the first ring from the front and the second ring from the back.

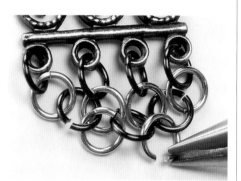

4 Add a ring in the same way between the second and third ring, then between the third and fourth. Three rings have been added to make this row.

5 To create your third row, using the same linking technique, add a ring linking the first and second rings of the last row and then another linking the second and third.

6 To keep the width of the piece even, hang another ring at each side of the previous row. There are four rings in this row.

Hanging your flat chain mail

You can hang your chain mail in various ways to create different looks.

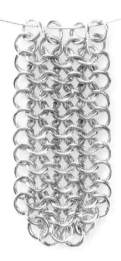

This piece is four rings wide on its larger row—remember you can use the same techniques to make chain mail of any width and length. If you hang your piece vertically the pattern is rather open.

7 Keep your chain lying flat as you work, continuing to link in new rings so that you have three rings in one row and four in the next. When the piece is the length that you require, finish with a four-ring row. Link these last four rings directly to the catch with one ring each. If you do not add this extra set of rings, the piece will not lie neatly as the last row and the loops on the catch are horizontal, so you need to add vertical links between them.

Section of flat chain mail attached to an elaborate clasp.

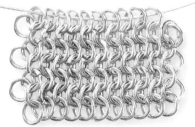

2 Try hanging the same piece from the side rings to create a much denser result.

Tubular chain mail

You can create tubular mail using the flat method (see page 62). Start with the piece of flat chain mail created on page 63 and add more rings to make your tube.

Tubular chain mail bracelet.

1 Start with a piece of flat chain mail with four ring and three ring rows (see page 63). You will have a piece of wire through your first row of jump rings. Add a jump ring into the outside ring on one side.

2 Now fold the piece of mail so that the two long edges meet. Link the new ring into the outside ring on the other side, exactly as you would link the two rings in a row on a flat piece.

3 Continue linking the side rings together with new rings until you reach the end of your piece of chain mail.

4 To add a clasp, add a second new ring into the last pair of side rings you connected, then another into the pair of rings at the opposite side of the tube. Here, a black jump ring has been used for visibility.

5 Then, using a 3 mm jump ring, add one into each of the other two end pairs to make the end more stable.

6 Use one more 3 mm jump ring to link the two larger end rings and the clasp together. Repeat at the other end of your tubular chain to add the other end of the clasp.

Tubular chain mail—tube method

Tubular chain mail can also be worked as a tube from the start, although this can be rather awkward, especially for the first few rows. It is much easier to work it around a cord as it gives you something to hold on to.

1 In this example, 4 mm jump rings made from 18 gauge (1 mm) wire and a 5 mm-thick cord are used. Start with four rings on a loop of wire that is large enough to fit around your cord.

2 Spread the rings out around your cord.

3 Now you can start to add rings, as you did in the first row of the flat chain mail (see page 62), linking each ring to the next.

4 Link the last ring on the wire to the first one, so you have formed a two-row circle of rings.

5 Continue in this way with four rings on every row until your piece is the required length. You can finish this tube as you did with the flat method tube (see opposite).

Tubular chain mail bracelet with cord.

DECORATING BEADS AND STONES

There are lots of ways that you can learn to wrap beads and decorate them with different wires. It is a great pleasure to be able to decorate quite a plain bead to make it very individual and special. Your skills in customizing your beads and stones will increase as your confidence in working with wire increases.

This section begins with some simple techniques, such as making beads that you can make from wire to use between other beads as spacers. This will help you to make your work more individual and will save you from having to buy huge amounts of beads every time you want to work on a project. You will also learn how to take one extra strand of wire across a bead, to help you to build up to some quite complex results, followed by building up your bead wrapping and coiling skills.

We have also covered some advanced techniques, for example, dealing with objects that don't have holes. You may have picked up a lovely stone from a beach or found a beautiful marble—if you practice the advanced techniques, you will be able to turn these into pendants or earrings.

WRAPPING A BEAD
HORIZONTALLY
see page 70

COILING AROUND
BEADS
see page 76

DOUBLE COIL
CAGED BEADS
see pages 78–79

ENCASING A
MARBLE
see page 82

WRAPPING A BEAD
VERTICALLY
see page 72

WRAPPING A BEAD
HORIZONTALLY
see page 70

WRAPPING
UNDRILLED PIECES
see page 80

WRAPPING A
CABOUCHON
see page 83

HORIZONTALLY
WRAPPED OPALINE
see page 70

ENCASED
MARBLE
see page 82

PARCEL-WRAPPED
AMBER
see page 81

WIRE-EDGED
PYRITE DONUT
see pages 74–75

Remember that you can also use the decorating skills in different contexts. If you cross reference this section with the Making findings section of the book (see page 26), you can use a lot of the techniques here to decorate the hooks or earwires featured there.

As with all the techniques that are covered in the book, try them, practice them, and then start to think laterally—you can make a herringbone wrap around a bead for a pendant, but you can also use the same wrap around the top of a bead ring (see page 109) or around a bead on an S-hook (see page 37). There lies the enjoyment of this section, plus the fact that you can make plain beads or found objects look great.

WRAPPING A
CABOUCHON
see page 83

PARCEL-WRAPPED
STONE
see page 81

HERRINGBONE
WRAPPING
see pages 72–73

HERRINGBONE
WRAPPING
see pages 72–73

SINGLE-WRAPPED
BEAD
see page 69

WRAPPING A BEAD
VERTICALLY
see page 72

DOUBLE COIL
CAGED BEAD
see pages 78–79

Wrapping beads

Assorted glass beads with a mixture of different spacer beads.

Embellishing quite plain beads by decorating them with a mixture of wires or with other beads looks very effective. A good place to start is to make some of your own beads to use as spacer beads.

Spacer beads

This is an area where you can really make use of your creative powers. You can make very precise, neat spacer beads or you can try adding lots of different wires for a much freer and more dramatic look.

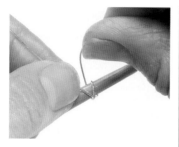

1 Try using a rounded chopstick. Allow plenty of wire. Leaving a tail of wire that you can hold onto, start to wrap the wire around the chopstick.

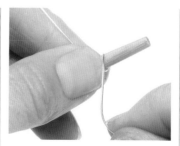

2 Wrap as neatly or crazily as you like but try to do your final wrap back onto the chopstick.

3 Slide the bead that you have made off the chopstick and trim off the end. Use a pair of pliers to tuck this end back inside the bead.

TOOLS

1 Wire cutters
2 Tubular object, such as a chopstick
3 Round-nose pliers
4 Chain-nose pliers

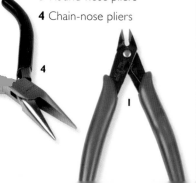

4 Finish by cutting off your first piece of wire. You should be able to almost clip back inside the bead so that there are no rough edges.

TIP **Remember that these techniques will all look different when made with different gauges of wire.**

Samples of beads.

Variations

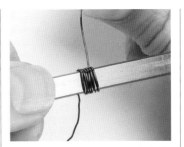

1 Try wrapping with two wires at the same time—you'll find that you get some really pretty mixed colors.

2 Try to make your wrapping into a rounder shape. This is easier to do around a narrower object, in this case a darning needle. Keep crisscrossing your wire, imagining that you are winding a ball of wool.

3 Experiment with winding onto other shapes, for example, a flat skewer, as above.

4 Try working with kinked wire. You can use up pieces that have become bent or you can wind some wire roughly round another tubular shape, then pull it off, stretch it out, and reuse it. You can even take this a stage further by using wire that you have wound on a Gizmo (see page 91). Stretch the wire out, then use it in the normal way. You can use your pliers to adjust the way the wire is sitting after you have made the bead.

Single-wrapped bead.

A single wrap across a bead

It's amazing how even the simplest techniques can make your beads look a little more special. Here, just a single strand of wire crossing a bead adds to its beauty.

1 You can use almost any sort of wire for this technique. You will need about 4 in. (10 cm) more than the length of your bead. Start by making a loop in the wire halfway along it. Make a couple of wraps above the loop and straighten the main wire.

2 Thread your bead onto the main wire. Now bring the other wire over the bead, keeping it as tight as you can. Start to make a couple of wraps above the bead. You may find it easier to use your chain-nose pliers to hold the wire as you do this.

3 Finish these wraps in the normal way by trimming off the end of the wire and smoothing it in. Add another bead above the wraps. Then make another loop with your main wire and wrap back down to the bead to finish.

TIP **Using the main bead and a smaller second bead, this technique works beautifully for pendants or earrings. If you are using it for bracelets or necklaces, remember to make a feature of the lack of symmetry.**

Single-wrapped agate beads and silver chain.

Wrapping a bead horizontally

This method of wrapping a bead is ideally suited to shapes with sharp edges. Go for square or rectangular beads rather than rounded ones, which are harder to work with.

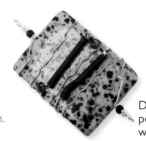

Dalmatian jasper pendant wrapped with two wires.

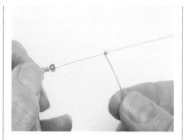

1 You need two lengths of wire: one to go through your bead about 3 in. (8 cm) longer than your bead and one to wrap with. The wrapping wire can be any sort but should be 22 gauge (0.6 mm) or finer. The length will depend on how many wraps you want to make or can fit on the bead—10 in. (25 cm) is used here. Start by making a closed loop at the bottom of your main wire and thread a small bead onto the wire.

2 Make a tiny spiral at the end of your wrapping wire by winding it with the tip of your round-nose pliers.

3 Now slide this onto your main wire. If the bead that you are threading has a large enough hole, you can slip the wrapping wire inside the bead.

4 Now bring the wrapping wire firmly up onto the bead and start to make your wraps, keeping them as tight as possible—you may feel as if you need an extra hand!

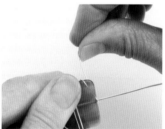

5 When you have completed your wraps, bring the wire back off the bead and wrap it around the main wire. Trim off the extra wire and smooth in as usual.

6 Add another small bead above the top of the wrapping wire and make a top loop in the usual way.

7 Now you can have fun. Use your chain-nose pliers to tighten the wrapping wire by placing them against the wire and making a small turn. This is called "angling" the wire. Be careful that you don't pull the wraps off the bead as you do it. Stop before you make the wire too tight in case you snap it and be careful not to scratch your bead as you do this.

Wrapped beads.

Variations

You can have more fun with your wrapping by adding small beads to the wrapping wire or by wrapping with several wires.

ADDING BEADS

1 Start as before, add your wrapping wire to your main wire. Then thread some small beads onto the wrapping wire. Now you can start to wrap as before but allowing some of the beads to slide down the wire so that they rest against the bead.

2 Finish off as before and angle the wire again to tighten it and position your beads.

Ceramic earrings wrapped with dark blue wire.

TIP **Remember that you can use these techniques with groups of beads too. For extra impact, try wrapping a multistrand bracelet with added wires and beads.**

Opaline pendant wrapped with crystals.

Triple-strand bracelet wrapped with wire and beads.

ADDING OTHER WIRES

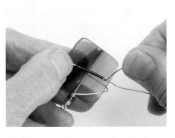

1 You can add a third wire by winding it round the wrapping wire before you start to wrap. The amount that you need will depend on whether you want a loose or tight wrap with the new wire. You may find it easier to wind the wire around a wire or narrow tubular object before threading it onto the wrapping wire.

2 You can also wrap the third wire on to the wrapping wire as you work. Finish as before and make any adjustments to position the extra wire on the wrapping wire.

Wrapping a bead vertically

A rounder bead is more challenging to wrap, but you can do so by taking your wires vertically onto the bead.

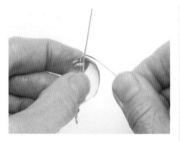

A vertically wrapped bead becomes a centerpiece for a necklace threaded on a beading wire.

1 Start as before, with a main wire to go through your bead. Add your wrapping wire in the same way as before; in this instance, 10 in. (25 cm) of wire is used to wrap a bead that is 1 in. (2.5 cm) long. Bring the wrapping wire up to the top and around the main wire.

2 Take the wire back to the bottom and round the main wire again and continue working up and down the bead. The design is your choice—you can cross the wires or work around the back if you wish to. Finish by taking the wrapping wire around the main one at the top and making a loop in that as before.

3 Now, if you like the look, you can angle the wires. You will have one more wrap on one side, so it is good to work one wire to the center.

TIP **Use your chain-nose pliers to pull up your main wire before making the top loop. It will make everything neater.**

Herringbone wrapping

This is a more structured version of vertical wrapping that highlights a bead very dramatically. It is also a lovely way to add a small bead to the S-hook shown on page 37. This technique is also used in the section on rings on page 108.

A Russian serpentine nugget with a herringbone wrap.

1 This technique requires considerably more main and wrapping wire. Here, the main wire is 7 in. (18 cm) long inside a bead that is ⅝ in. (15 mm) long. The wrapping wire is 16 in. (40 cm) long. Start by making a loop in the main wire, about one third of the way from one end. Make plenty of wraps above this loop—as many as eight or nine.

2 Thread your bead onto the wire and make another loop above it, leaving enough space for you to make the same number of wraps above the bead as below.

More random vertical wrapping, with crossing wires on both sides of this bead.

3 Wind your new wire around the top of the bead, leaving a short tail so that you can hold it in place. Now start your herringbone wrap. If you are making a pendant, remember to have the top loop sideways onto you. Curve the wire around beside the bead.

4 Work around the main wire beneath the bead, making your wrapping wire cross at the front. Take it back up to the top on the other side of the bead. Trim off the tail of the wrapping wire once you feel it is secure.

TIP **The secret to success is to keep the wire curved out to the side as you wrap. Try wrapping in different directions and consider the different effects you have achieved.**

A horn bead showing a variation in wrapping, with the wire crossed at the top in front and at the bottom in back.

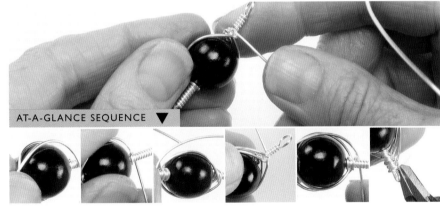

AT-A-GLANCE SEQUENCE ▼

5 Take the wrapping wire around the main wire at the top, again having it cross in front.

6 Continue in this way, gently working back up the wrapping loops that you made on each end of your main wire. When you have reached each end of your main wire, cut off the last bit of the wrapping wire and smooth in the end. Your bead will look different on either side.

Decorating donuts

You can make very impressive pendants by adding wire and perhaps some small beads to a donut. There are many different ways to wrap them: here are two simple ideas. You can hang your donut from a fairly thick wire, then use a thinner one to decorate it.

Wraps and coils

This method uses a loose wire with coiled ends.

1 Use a 20 gauge (0.8 mm) wire to make a loop that your donut will hang from (see page 21).

2 For the wrapping, take a very generous piece of 22 gauge (0.6 mm) wire. Make a coil in one end of this wire (see page 44).

3 Hold the coil against the donut, then start to work the rest of the wire through the central hole and on around the sides.

TOOLS

1 Wire cutters
2 Chain-nose pliers
3 Wide-nose pliers
4 Acrylic-nosed pliers for the coils
(optional)

4

4 It helps to keep the loop as wide as possible while you are positioning the wraps, then pull them as tight as possible.

5 When you have completed the wraps, coil the last length of the wire down onto the donut. You can then use your chain-nose pliers to angle the wire and tighten it onto the donut (see Wrapping a bead horizontally, page 70).

Plain wire-edged donut.

Creating a wire edging

This is another very effective way to make more of a donut. It may require a little bit of practice but will be well worth the effort.

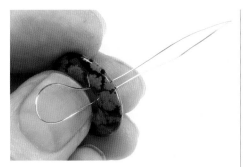

1 You will find it much easier to practice this technique with a very soft wire. For a small donut, try 16 in. (40 cm) of 28 gauge (0.3 mm) wire. Make a curve in the wire several centimeters in from the end. Hold this against the donut with both ends coming through the center.

2 Take both ends up the back of the donut and through the curve in the wire, then pull the ends up firmly.

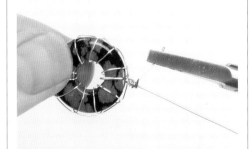

3 Make a large loop in the wire to the right of this first wrap and bring the end of the wire through it. This will make your next wrap. Repeat steps 2 and 3, working around the donut. Try to keep the wraps evenly spaced. If wished, you can add beads to the wire as you bring it up the front of the donut.

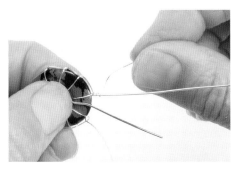

4 Leave a gap after the last wrap and change to a heavier wire on which you will hang the donut. Fold the wire around the donut and wind your wrapping wires round the back of it, trimming them off and smoothing them in.

5 Now wrap the short end of your hanging wire above the wires that you have just smoothed in, then add a bead and make your top loop as usual. You can angle the wires on the front of the donut if you wish to, but be careful that you don't sheer the fine wire.

TIP **If you don't get your wrap tight enough, put your pliers into the wrap in the center of the donut and release the tension on the wire so that you can pull it again and get it tighter.**

Coiling around beads

Coiling down a bead from both ends adds embellishment and creates a unique chain-link component.

This example is worked with a 10 mm round bead and 20 gauge (0.8 mm) silver-plated wire. For this size of bead, cut 12 in. (30 cm) of wire and thread the bead so that it is about 1 in. (2.5 cm) from the middle.

Silver-coiled beads can be used as pendants or earrings, or they can be combined with other plain and decorated beads to create lavish chains (as shown above). It's important to use as round a bead as possible: if the bead has slightly flattened ends the wire won't coil around it successfully and the coils will tend to sit on top rather than beside each other. You will find it easier to practice with a reasonably heavy wire so that the coils have some substance and can hold their shape.

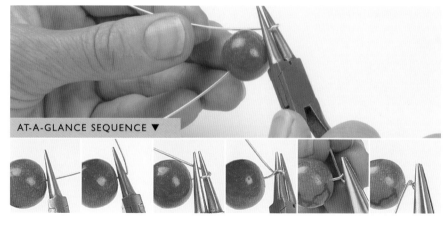

AT-A-GLANCE SEQUENCE ▼

2 Make a loop on one side with your round-nose pliers. Then, holding the loop with your chain-nose pliers, wrap the end of the wire three times around itself. Don't cut off this length of wire.

TOOLS

1 Wire cutters

2 Round-nose pliers

3 Chain-nose pliers

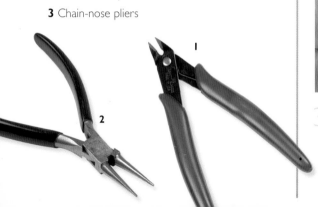

3 Push the bead close to these wraps and move the end of the wire away from the bead.

4 Place your pliers on the wire on the other side of the bead to make a space for three wraps here.

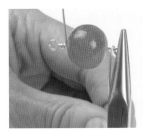

5 Make three wraps around the wire on this side, while holding the loop securely with the chain-nose pliers.

6 Keep winding the wire around the bead. Move your hands away from the bead to hold the wire and guide it slightly toward the center of the bead as you coil.

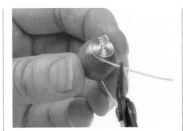

7 Either cut off the end of the wire very close to the bead or leave enough length to make a tiny loop in the end.

8 If you are making a loop, place the tips of your round-nose pliers around the end of the wire and curl it back toward the coils that you have made.

9 Now move to the other side. Reposition your wire so that it now angles toward the bead. Start to coil around this side of the bead.

10 As before, keep wrapping until you run out of wire or lose the shape of the coil.

11 When you have finished the coiling on this side, cut the end of the wire and finish it as you finished the other side.

TIP **Keep the wire moving and don't pull too firmly. Stop when you run out of wire or when the coil begins to lose shape.**

Perfectly round beads are the best kind for coiling.

Advanced wrapping techniques

Most of these techniques require a little more patience but will bring great rewards, since nearly all can be used with objects other than beads.

Wrapping objects without holes

One of the great advantages of working with wire is that you can combine it with items other than beads, that don't have holes. You may be tempted by pieces of sea glass, marbles, or undrilled pieces of stone. These are a few of the techniques that you can try.

Caged marble earrings.

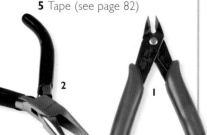

DOUBLE COIL CAGES
The only complicated aspect of these cages is getting your measurements right. As with so many other techniques, you need to cut a piece of inexpensive wire, keep a record of its length, then experiment.

For the caging to work well, you need a fairly heavy-gauge wire. Here, 14 in. (35 cm) of 20 gauge (0.8 mm) wire is wrapped around a ⅝ in. (15 mm) marble. Start by making a coil (see page 44) in each end of the wire. They should face in opposite directions and need to meet in the middle, so either mark the middle of your wire or coil from both ends at the same time so that the coils are the same size.

2 When both your coils reach the middle, fold them in half and squeeze them gently together.

3 Now, using your pliers, ease the inner loops from each end of the coils. Then use two pairs of pliers to gently open up the coils.

4 Now work the marble between the coils and arrange them around it. These pieces can be attached to an earwire for almost instant earrings, or linked together to form a chain.

TIP **As the coils will be large ones, use acrylic pliers as these are less likely to mark the wire.**

Variation

This also makes a lovely and quite quick way of wrapping beads. You can either ignore the fact that they have holes and use the loops on the coils to connect your pieces, or you can run another wire through the beads.

Chain of dichroic glass pieces.

1 Make the double coils exactly as you did in the previous technique and work your bead into the center. Carefully trim the loops off at each end.

2 Now you can insert another wire through the bead and the cage. Thread more beads onto this wire, finishing with a closed loop.

Caged foil-bead earrings.

Caging groups of beads

When wrapping is talked about we tend to think about individual beads or interesting objects, but making a spiral for a group of beads is also very effective. You need to work with quite sturdy wires for this as there will be space between them and the beads.

1 You will be wrapping the wire around a tubular object and the beads will go inside this, so hunt around to find something that is a suitable size, such as this fat marker pen. Wind the wire firmly around it.

2 Remove the spiral of wire, cut the end off, then cut it in half. Use your round-nose pliers to make a small loop in each end of both spirals.

3 Make a closed loop in the end of another wire and thread this through your beads and the wire spiral. You may want to readjust the angle of the loops in the spirals when you have seen how they sit. Now you can add an earwire to make earrings.

TIP **You can vary this method by coiling stiff wire around an object and adding beads to the wire for a crazy spiral of color— it's a good way to create maximum impact with inexpensive beads (see below).**

Wrapping unusual pieces

The most difficult undrilled objects to wrap are smooth and round—Double coil cages on page 78 suggests one way of working with them. Items that are rougher and more uneven are easier to deal, such as the pieces of amber on these pages. Suggestions are given for how to work with them or pieces like them.

WRAPPING AROUND A CENTRAL WIRE

This is a good way to wrap a piece if you are happy for it to hang horizontally.

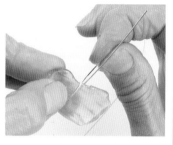

1 For all of these techniques, allow plenty of wire for your wrapping and a wire that isn't too heavy a gauge. In this example, leave a length of wire at the back of the piece of amber. Bring the rest of the wire round the amber and back up to wrap round this wire.

2 Keep wrapping around the amber, choosing the most secure-looking places so that your wire doesn't slide off. Take each wrap round the central wire.

3 When you feel that you have enough wraps to hold the piece of amber securely, take your wrapping wire around the straight wire to finish it.

Plain wrapped undrilled amber.

4 Now you can add a bead and finish with a top loop.

5 You can angle the wrapping wire to tighten it, but be careful not to pull the wrapping wire off the edges of your amber.

Wrapped amber with some extra beads and wire.

Amber wrapped
with wires crossed
at the back.

PARCEL WRAPPING

This is a way to wrap when you want your piece
to hang vertically.

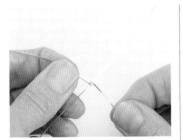

1 Cut two pieces of wire and
wind one around the other,
three-quarters of the way
along the wire.

2 Take the longer wire around
the bottom of the amber and
bring it back up the other side.

3 Bring one of the horizontal
pieces of wire round to the
back and press all your wires
firmly against the amber. Now
you can mark where you want
this wire to finish.

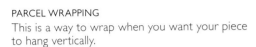

4 Take the wire off the amber and
carefully wrap the horizontal
wire in the place that you
have marked. Cut off the end
of this wire.

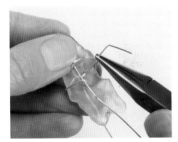

5 Put the amber back into the
cage that you are making.
Then bring the other horizontal
wire round to the back and
wrap that one round the main
wire too.

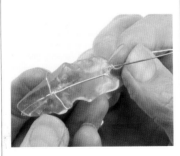

6 You can then wrap the vertical
wire at the front around the
wire that stands up at the back
of your piece. Add a bead and
finish, again angling the wire
to tighten if you want to.

TIP **You can also
parcel wrap by just
crossing the wires
at the back of the
piece (see above),
but if you don't
have a wire running
up the front it
is likely to fall
forward a little
when it is hanging.**

Two parcel-wrapped
pieces of amber, one
with extra coils.

Encasing a marble

A marble is used to demonstrate this technique, but you could try this method with other undrilled pieces.

Encased marble
on suede thong.

1 Cut two lengths of wire: two 8 in. (20 cm) lengths of 24 gauge (0.5 mm) wire. You will also need another 2 ½ in. (6 cm) for the bottom wrap. Place the two wires side by side and wrap the short wire around the middle of them. Trim and press in the ends of the short wire.

2 Press the wrap under the marble and bring the lengths of long wire up the sides. Then use tape to secure them to the sides of the marble.

3 Cross the wires at the top of the marble so that you can make a hanger directly above the wrap at the bottom. Bend one pair of wires up with your chain-nose pliers.

Encased marbles—you could add earwires to make beautiful earrings.

4 Ease the other pair of wires around the bottom of the first pair, so that they wrap close to the marble. Make a couple of turns, then trim off the excess wire.

5 Put a bead above these wraps and carefully make a top loop with your remaining wires as you would for any closed loop (see page 18).

6 Now begin to draw the wires out around the marble as you remove the tape so that the marble is securely held. You can use your chain-nose pliers to "angle" the wire around the marble to remove any slack and to decorate the marble some more.

Wrapping a cabouchon

This works in a very similar way to the encased marble. It is another approach to working with an item that doesn't have a hole. This method works better with a flatter object and is especially good if you want to draw attention to the front of the object.

Wrapped dichroic glass cabouchons.

1 Start as you did with the encased marble on page 82, but this time you are working with three long wires and three short wires. Wrap the shorter wires round the long ones. Trim off the middle wires and squeeze the ends against the long wires, making sure they are in the middle. You can leave the ends on the other two wires if you want to decorate with them later.

2 Draw all the wires firmly around the cabouchon and tape them into place as firmly as you can. You may want to open the bottom wires a little before you do this to create a little cradle for the cabouchon.

3 Spread the wires around the cabouchon a little at the top, without removing the tape. When everything is in place, use your chain-nose pliers to bend up the wires above the cabouchon. Now use a piece of scrap wire to hold the tops of the wire together.

4 Trim off four of the long wires, two on either side, just above where you have wrapped the temporary wire.

5 Using the last two wires, make a top loop and wrap them back down to the cabouchon, unwrapping the temporary wire as you work. You can either trim the ends of these wires off or leave them to make decorative coils.

6 Now remove the tape and pull the side wires further around the cabouchon to secure it firmly. You can "angle" the wires with your chain-nose pliers to tighten them.

7 Finally, for a more decorative effect, coil the ends of the side and top wires if wished.

KNIT AND TWIST TECHNIQUES

Another interesting way in which to use wire is to create knitted and twisted work. This is mostly done with much finer wire and you can work with and without the addition of beads.

KNITTED WIRE POD NECKLACES
see pages 86 and 149

Most of the techniques shown in this section are very simple, but it does help if you can knit and crochet. This section has a different feel to most of the others in the book, and if you are already good at conventional knitting or crochet you will very quickly be able to add your skills to the basics that are shown here. But if you have never knitted, you will be surprised at how easy it is to get exciting results when you are using wires. Making a pair of earrings or a bracelet cuff isn't going to take you nearly as long as it takes to knit a sweater!

The basics of French knitting are also covered. Again you can create interesting pieces of jewelry by practicing with this and discovering the different results that you can achieve.

Before you start to use the techniques that are shown in this section, it is a good idea to look at the wire gauge chart shown on page 11. You should work with very fine wires—28 gauge (0.3 mm) or 30 gauge (0.2 mm) wires. You can also try using recycled wires such as fuse wire to see how this affects the outcome.

KNITTED EARRINGS WITH BEADS
see page 86

FRENCH KNITTING WITH ADDED BEADS
see page 87

FRENCH KNITTING WITH BEADS ENCASED
see page 87

CROCHET WITH BEADS
see page 88

KNITTED WIRE AND BEADS PRESSED TOGETHER AND WORKED ONTO CHAINS
see pages 86 and 149

RANDOM BEAD
BRACELET WRAPPED
WITH TWISTED WIRES
see page 89

TWISTED WIRE JUMP
RING BRACELET

The twisting part of this section is also great fun—just using your fingers to combine the wires together to create crazy pieces of jewelry. Again, once you have learned the techniques, you can try using them in different ways. For example, a tiara is featured in the Constructing with wire section on page 116—using twisted wire would be another great way to interpret the design.

While you are trying the techniques that are shown here, keep thinking of all of the different possibilities. Would this piece of knitting look good with beads added? Should they be every row or every other row? Would it be exciting to press or "scrunch" the pieces of knitting together? How about knitting with something slightly larger? It is up to you to explore and enjoy the techniques you have learned.

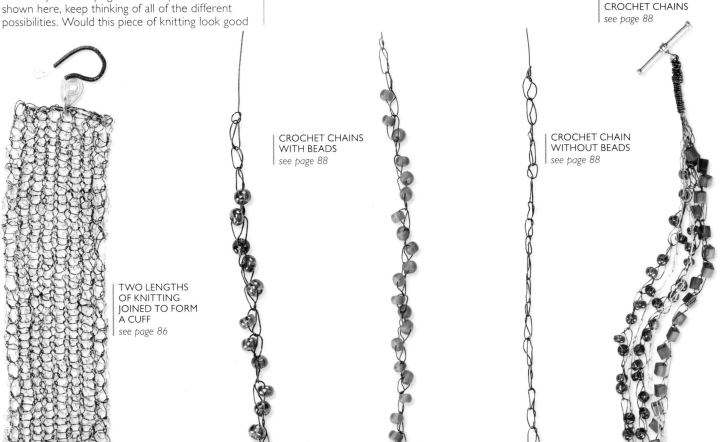

TWO LENGTHS
OF KNITTING
JOINED TO FORM
A CUFF
see page 86

CROCHET CHAINS
WITH BEADS
see page 88

CROCHET CHAIN
WITHOUT BEADS
see page 88

BRACELET MADE WITH
CROCHET CHAINS
see page 88

Knitting and crochet techniques

In this section, some of the techniques that would traditionally be worked with threads are used with fine wires.

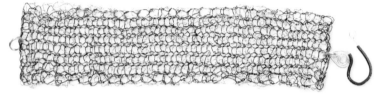

Bracelet made from two sewn-together lengths of knitting.

Knitting

You can try knitting with all sorts of different implements. You are likely to be making quite narrow bands of work, so try with fine knitting needles, darning needles, or even cocktail sticks. You will find that you need wire that is 28 gauge (0.3 mm) or finer.

1 The wire used here is 30 gauge (0.2 mm) wire. Start by making a loop in the wire, leaving a tail that you can use when finishing your work. Cast on more stitches by making loops over your finger and transferring them onto your needle. Make enough stitches to give you the width of band you want.

2 Now you can start to knit. You will be working in plain knitting, building up your rows. The success of your knitting will be based on keeping everything loose as you work: you will pull it into shape later. Resist the temptation to wind the wire around your finger as you work as this may make it kink.

3 Your first few rows will look very messy, but the band will begin to take shape as you work. Just count your number of stitches from time to time to make sure that you haven't dropped one along the way, and keep knitting.

4 When you reach the required length, take your knitting off the needle and work the end of your wire through the stitches, using a needle if easier. If making a bracelet, you can bring the ends back to the middle of the row at each end and attach a fastener; or work them in and attach a clasp with jump-rings.

KNITTING WITH BEADS
This technique is worked in the same way as above, but you thread your beads onto the wire before you start knitting.

Knitted earrings with beads on every row.

1 Cast on your stitches as before and work a row without beads to start. In the next row add a bead between each stitch.

2 Decide whether to have beads on every row or every other row. If making a bracelet, beads on every other row will create a smoother surface to go against your wrist. Finish off with a row of knitting without beads to match the first row.

French knitting

You may remember doing French knitting as a child. Now there is a version that can be used with wire and with beads. The knitting spools are larger than the ones that you may remember and are supplied with a stylus tool to manipulate the wire. Try experimenting with different gauges of wire: 28 gauge (0.3 mm) or finer will be the most suitable. You can use the tubes of knitting on their own as chains, or try putting beads of a suitable size in the middle of them for a fascinating effect. You can also add beads as you work to make the chain more complex.

Bracelet of French knitting with beads added as it is worked.

AT-A-GLANCE SEQUENCE ▼

A chain of wire with glass beads captured within it. Threads are added and run through the tubing to complete the necklace.

Insert a length of wire down through the center of the spool—you need this tail of wire so that you can pull your work down with it. Now start to load the pegs by winding your wire clockwise around them, working counterclockwise around the spool.

2 Start your first row of knitting by placing your wire across the next peg. It helps to bring the wire on through behind the next peg. Use the stylus (or knitting needle) to reach down and lift the bottom loop on the peg over the new wire.

3 Continue to work in this way, moving round and round the spool, pulling the knitting down from below as it progresses.

4 You can add suitable beads to the center of your knitting as you work (see necklace above). To finish, cut the wire and take it through a loop, then take the loop off the peg. Work your way around all the pegs, binding off the loops. Pull the wire tight.

FRENCH KNITTING WITH BEADS

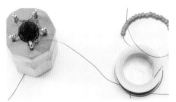

If you are working with beads, thread them onto your wire before you load your spool.

2 Start with a few rows of plain knitting, then allow a bead to move into place before working the next peg. Keep adding a bead before making each loop.

3 Draw your work down to check that the beads and wire will fit comfortably into the tube. Finish with a few rows of plain knitting and bind off as before.

Bracelet of crochet chains with and without beads.

Crochet

You can use fine wires to create a chain of crocheted wire. As with knitting, you can make the chain with or without beads. Try experimenting with 28, 30, or 32 gauge (0.3, 0.2, or 0.1 mm) wire.

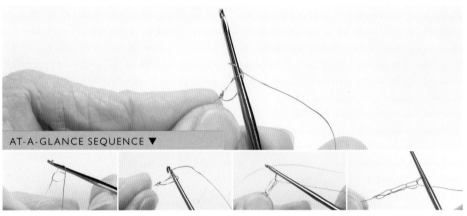

AT-A-GLANCE SEQUENCE ▼

To make a simple chain, start by making a loop, leaving a tail of wire that you can hold in your left hand. Put your crochet hook through the loop, take the wire around the hook, and draw it back through the loop. Continue to add loops in this way.

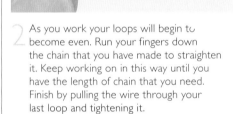

2 As you work your loops will begin to become even. Run your fingers down the chain that you have made to straighten it. Keep working on in this way until you have the length of chain that you need. Finish by pulling the wire through your last loop and tightening it.

CROCHETING WITH BEADS
You can also add beads to your crocheted chains.

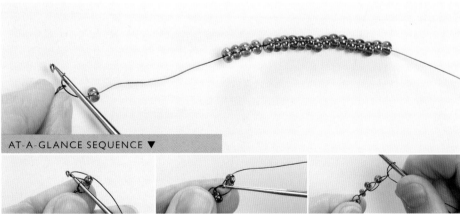

AT-A-GLANCE SEQUENCE ▼

Thread your beads onto your wire, then proceed as for a simple chain. Begin to add the beads by letting them move along the wire and drop into place before you make each loop. Give the chain a pull to get the beads into place.

Crochet chains with and without beads.

Twisting techniques

You can add to your skills by spending some time twisting wires. You can do this by hand, adding beads as you work to create freehand sculptural pieces such as brooches, tiaras, bracelets, or chokers. Or you can learn to use tools that twist wires to add more texture to your work.

Pendant made from twisted square wire around a simple bead.

Twisting a single wire

You can twist square or triangular wire by using a pin vise and a clamp, or a pair of pin vises.

1 | Push the end of your wire into the pin vise and tighten the vise.

2 | Secure the other end of the wire. Use a clamp, as here, or if you are twisting only a short length try holding one end of the wire with chain-nose pliers.

AT-A-GLANCE SEQUENCE ▼

3 | Now twist the wire loosely or tightly dependent on your design. To finish, cut off the ends of the wire, then file them.

Twisting two wires

1 | You can twist two wires together in exactly the same way as for a single wire. Just force both wires into your pin vise and secure the other end as before.

2 | Use your pliers to remove the twisted wires from the pin vise.

3 | File the ends to make them neat.

2

FREEHAND TWISTING

You can have great fun twisting wires by hand, as long as the wire isn't too heavy. This is a great technique for making tiaras and can also be used for other sorts of jewelry.

Freehand twisted wire bracelet.

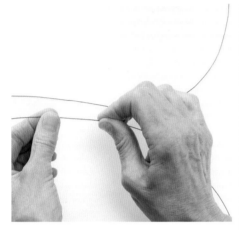

1 | Try working with two 24 gauge (0.5 mm) wires, each 24 in. (60 cm) long, and a handful of beads. You can work along from one end or start in the middle of your wires.

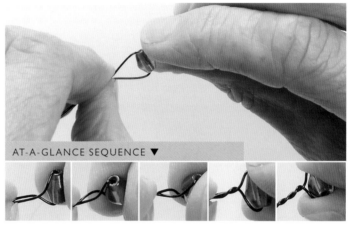

AT-A-GLANCE SEQUENCE ▼

2 | Thread a bead onto a wire and use your fingers to twist the wire together to make a stem.

TIP **You can add extra wire if you run short—just join the wires beneath the beads.**

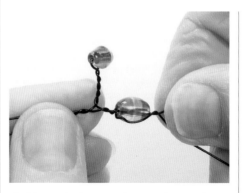

3 | Now twist the two wires together, maybe with another bead added to create a space between the beads.

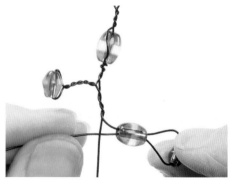

4 | Add another bead—it can be on the other side of the wires to create a stem on this side too. Now you can have fun working in a random or organized way. To finish, wind the ends onto a fastener.

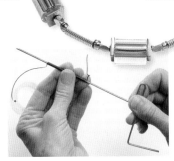

Bracelet with simple spiral and furnace beads.

Using a Gizmo

A Gizmo is a tool that was devised to make neat spirals of wire. You could wind wire around a tubular object to create the spirals, but the Gizmo will save a lot of time. Use these spirals in different ways in your designs.

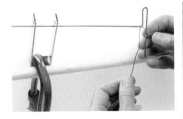

1 Clamp your Gizmo to a table and attach the wire to one of the rods.

2 Then wind the handle to twist the wire, keeping it running smoothly to create a neat spiral that isn't too tight.

3 When you have a suitable length, cut the attaching wire and slide the spiral off the rod. Make sure you have neat cuts at the ends of the spiral.

MAKING GIZMO BEADS

You can make a wide range of different-shaped beads with a Gizmo. This is a basic one to try as a starter. Experiment with different combinations of gauges and colors, and with both sizes of rod.

1 Make a spiral of wire as before. Then thread this onto another wire. Now attach the inner wire to one of the rods of the Gizmo.

2 Turn the rod a few times with only the plain wire, then start to wind the spiral of wire as well.

3 Finish by winding the plain wire a couple of times and remove the spiral from the rod. Tidy the ends.

4 Now try reshaping the spiral. Here, it is being wound clockwise with the right hand and counterclockwise with the left hand, but you can try other variations.

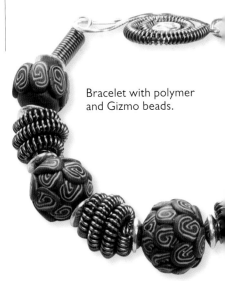

5 Use pliers to tuck in the outer lengths of wire for a neat finish.

Bracelet with polymer and Gizmo beads.

CONSTRUCTING WITH WIRE

This section of the book covers the more structural ways of using wire, including ways to make bracelets, hoop earrings, brooches, rings, and pendants. A tiara has been included as an introduction to making wedding jewelry.

In explaining some basic ideas for these pieces of jewelry, the pieces in this section are shown in step-by-step format. Once you have mastered the version that is shown here, you should use the featured designs as templates and adapt them for use with the beads that you have and the jewelry that you want to achieve.

Some of the structures that follow are free-form, and some are more ordered. Some work several different types of wire together in the same piece.

Most require patience and confident handling of the wires that you are working with, but your end results will be unique and stunning. And you are still working with fairly simple tools and without the need for heating the wires or using chemicals.

Guidance has been given for the gauges of wire that you will need for the different design ideas. You may find that it makes sense to try making some of the pieces in a lighter wire and then move to a heavier one as you feel more confident. Once you

BEAD RING WITH WRAPPING
see page 109

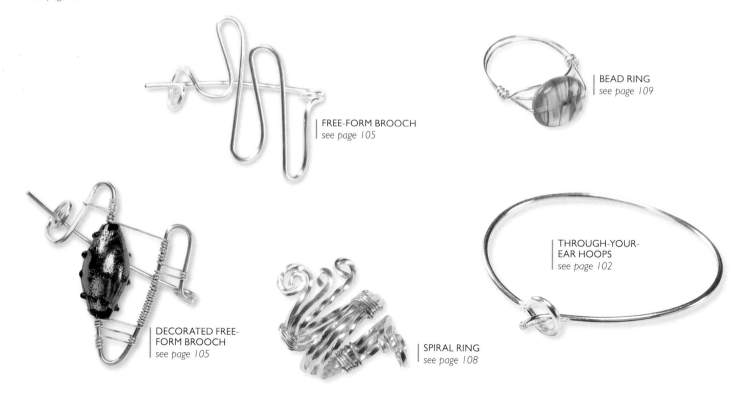

FREE-FORM BROOCH
see page 105

BEAD RING
see page 109

DECORATED FREE-FORM BROOCH
see page 105

SPIRAL RING
see page 108

THROUGH-YOUR-EAR HOOPS
see page 102

**WORKING IN TWO
DIRECTIONS**
see page 94

LADDER BRACELET
see page 98

become more assured you will probably find that you want to move to using sterling silver wire or even gold, so that the effort that you have made will be more long lasting. Sizing is more important when you are making rings and bangles—again this can be helped by making a practice piece and keeping a careful note of the measurements.

Memory wire is a very different type of wire and can only be manipulated a very small amount—a design idea using it is featured in this section. It is strong and can be a very good base to build on. Remember the warning about not using delicate tools with it (see page 96), and be careful, since it is very sharp.

Once you have tried making the rings and bangles shown in this section, you might feel inspired to extend your jewelry-making skills by looking at the Toward silversmithing section (see page 118).

**USING WIRE TO THREAD
AND SPACE BEADS**
see page 95

HOOP EARRINGS
see page 103

SIMPLE BANGLE
see page 99

DOUBLE BANGLE
see page 100

Simple techniques

Chain of glass flower beads with a hanging central bead.

This section of the book begins with a few simple ideas to extend the possibilities of using beads and wires together.

Working in two directions

You can use this technique when you want to connect your beads in two different directions. It works well as a centerpiece for a dramatic necklace or, on a smaller scale, it can make some striking earrings.

TIP **You can put your pliers back into the bottom loop to reposition it a little.**

TOOLS

1 Wire cutters

2 Round-nose pliers

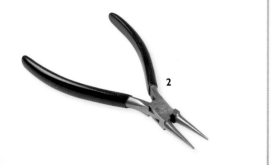

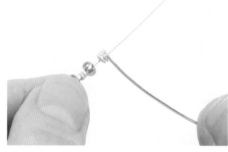

You will need two wires, one to go through the bead and one to wrap round it. This example is worked with 4 ¾ in (12 cm) of 20 gauge (0.8 mm) wire for each wire. Start by making a closed loop in one end of one of the wires and adding a small bead. Now attach your second wire to it. You can either do this by wrapping the new wire round the first, or you can use your round-nose pliers to make a small spiral in the new wire, which you will thread on to the first wire.

2 Thread on your main bead then curve your second wire firmly below it so that you can find the center.

3 Roll the wire back with your round-nose pliers so that you create a loop below the bead.

4 Curve the wire around to the other side and wrap it back onto the wire that runs through the bead. You can finish this with another small bead and another loop. You can also use the bottom loop to hang other pieces.

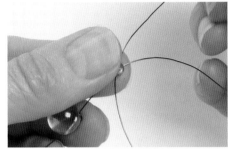

Using wire to thread and space beads

Fine wires work wonderfully as a way to space beads for a single or multistrand design bracelet or necklace. This is an easy way to use wire to get a dramatic result from your beads.

A necklace of "off-center" drilled glass beads and wire.

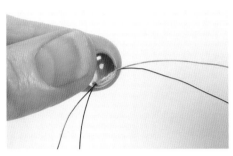

1 First work out how much wire you will need for each strand of your design—you should allow at least double the length of the strand that you want to make. You should also take into account the size of your beads and the spaces between them. The necklace here is 18 in. (45 cm) long and uses 36 in. (90 cm) of 30 gauge (0.3 mm) wire. Start in the center of wire, threading on a bead and then taking the wire through the hole a second time.

2 Pull the wire firmly, smoothing it against the bead so that it is held neatly in place.

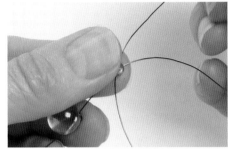

3 Now, working in exactly the same way, add more beads on either side of the first one, leaving a space between them. Continue adding beads to build your design.

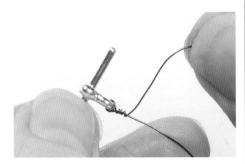

4 You can finish the strands by wrapping them singly or in groups onto a fastener.

TIP **You can create great designs with this technique using mixed bags of beads.**

A simple bracelet made from wired, spaced beads.

Using memory wire

Memory wire is a strange product to work with. It has to be treated as a threading material rather than something that can be manipulated. However, it can be used to great effect as a core to build on. Be very careful when you work with memory wire, making sure that you don't use your good, delicate tools with it as you will damage them. You can use heavier pliers to start with, then, if you find you like memory wire, buy a pair of memory-wire cutters. Here are two quick ideas to introduce you to working with this wire.

Bracelet of mixed beads on memory wire.

Simple winding bracelet

This couldn't be easier and is a great way to use up mixed bags of beads.

1 Cut or buy a bracelet length of memory wire; you will need enough for about three complete loops of wire.

2 With your round-nose pliers, roll a loop in one end of the wire.

3 Keep threading on the beads until all three loops of wire are full, but leaving just enough wire to roll a small loop at the other end.

TOOLS

1 Memory-wire cutters
2 Heavy round-nose pliers

TIP **Be VERY careful when working with memory wire as it is sharp and can easily scratch you.**

Double-strand memory wire bracelet

You can use memory wire to create the core of this double strand bracelet. It will work well with the dumbbell spacers on page 51.

Double Dalmatian jasper bracelet.

1 Make some spacers for your bracelet—these ones are the dumbbell shown on page 51. Cut two lengths of memory wire to go around your wrist.

2 Roll up one end of each wire. Start to thread your beads, adding your spacer bars as you work.

3 At the end of the bracelet, trim the wires back a little if you need to, then roll these ends into loops.

4 You can add a small piece of chain and a fastener into the rolled loops of the bracelet.

TIP **You can wrap a bracelet like this with more wire and beads. Look at the example on page 79 (wrapping groups of beads).**

Bracelets and bangles

You can make a range of bracelets by linking beads together or making chains, as shown previously. The ideas presented here will extend the scope of how you use wires for very different designs.

Ladder bracelet with tube beads.

Ladder bracelet

This simple idea involves linking two pieces of chain with fairly sturdy wire—thin enough to slot through the links in the chain—then decorating the wire with beads to create a bracelet. By altering your choice of beads and chains you can create a range of different looks.

1 Use 20 gauge (0.8 mm) wire. The length depends on the length of the beads; you'll need about 1 in. (2 ½ cm) for the turns outside the chains. Join both chains at one end with your fastener. Then fold over one end of the wire with chain-nose pliers, and squeeze.

2 Flick the fold over a second time and squeeze again.

3 Now work through a link in the chain. Start at a point that will allow your fastener to have some movement. Thread the bead onto the wire and work through the corresponding link on the other chain.

4 Trim the wire so that you have just over ½ in. (1 cm) left. Repeat the folding process on the other side of the chain, bending the wire back toward it.

TOOLS

1 Wire cutters

2 Chain-nose pliers

3 Mandrel or tubular object (see page 99)

4 File (see page 99)

5 Round-nose pliers

6 Masking tape (see page 100)

7 Wide-nose pliers (see page 101)

5 Continue building the sections between the pieces of chain, leaving enough space between them so that they sit well together. When your bracelet is long enough, finish by putting the other end of your fastener onto the chain.

TIP **If you are unhappy with any of the links, you can easily change them when the bracelet is finished.**

To keep your bangle secure make sure that your hook is a tight fit with the loop on its other side.

Simple bangle

There are many ways that you can use heavier wires to create bangles and bracelets. Try starting with a simple design using a single wire. This can be embellished with wrapping or elaborate hooks. All of the tools that you use with heavier-gauge wires should be heavier too—save your delicate wire cutters and small round-nose pliers to use with the thinner wires.

Simple bangle of glass and silver beads with a simple S-hook.

1 Cut a length of 18 gauge (1.25 mm) wire: you will need to allow extra length to accommodate the diameter of the beads that you will thread onto it. Curve your wire around a triblett or mandrel, but you can experiment with other tubular objects. This is a tube of plastic that is about the size of a wrist.

2 File one end of the wire. Bend it toward you a little, then roll it against the rest of the wire with your round-nose pliers.

3 Now add your beads or decorate your wire, leaving a tail of wire about ¾ in. (2 cm) long to make your other loop.

4 File the wire tail. Then draw the wire toward you a bit and roll it away with your round-nose pliers.

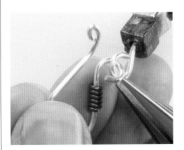

5 Add a hook of your choice to fasten your bracelet (see pages 35–41). Open one of your loops sideways to position the hook.

Polymer and silver beads with a coil hook.

Double bangle

Another approach for a slightly sturdier bangle is to double your wire. You can use this method to create a bracelet that will have a hook as part of the structure. Again it will be better to use heavier tools for these techniques.

Crystal double-wrapped bracelet.

1 Cut a length of 18 gauge (1 mm) or 20 gauge (0.8 mm) wire. You are likely to need about 18 in. (46 cm). Measure a little way along the length of your wire and turn it back on itself, using a wide part of your pliers so that you create a space between the two lengths.

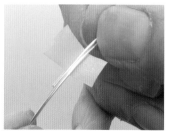

2 Smooth the lengths together and hold them tightly with masking tape.

3 Straighten out the rest of the wire, then fold the other end back tightly on to itself, using your pliers so that the two ends of the wire just touch. Again tape this into place.

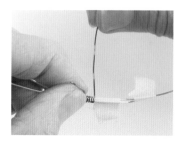

4 Now cut a long length of a wrapping wire. You could use a colored wire, a half-hard 22 gauge (0.6 mm) wire or finer. Or try a half-circular wrapping wire. Start wrapping your core wires about ¾ in. (2 cm) from one end.

5 Work along the double wire, removing the masking tape as you go and wrapping over the joining ends of the wire.

6 Stop wrapping about 1 ¼ in. (3 cm) from the other end of the wires. Then ease your structure around a tubular object. The ideal object is a mandrel, but try anything else that is very strong.

7 Bend back the tightly folded end of the bangle to form a hook. Then flick up the end of the hook.

TIP **You can add beads as you wrap the bangle, or to make it even sturdier you can rewrap it and add beads at that stage.**

Multiwire bangle

You can make your bracelets and bangles even more complex by wiring several strands together. This bracelet has a double frame with one strand of wire in the middle, but the idea could be adapted to hold many strands of wire. The wire here has been woven between the strands; an alternative would be to make flat wraps.

Woven wire and dichroic bead bracelet.

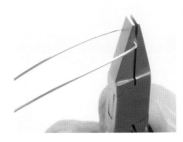

1 For this bracelet, you need 18 in. (45 cm) of 20 gauge (0.8 mm) wire. Mark the middle of the wire and fold the wire over your wide-nose pliers to make a flat end for your bracelet.

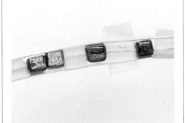

2 Cut another length of 20 gauge (0.8 mm) wire about 7 in. (18 cm) long. Choose some beads that will fit on this wire inside your main wire. Start to build the central pattern of the bracelet by positioning masking tape to hold everything in place.

3 Cut a length of wire to weave between the other wires: a 24 gauge (0.5 mm) wire has been used here. Starting beside your central bead, wind this weaving wire round one of the outer wires. Leave a little tail to hold this wire steady.

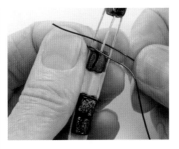

4 Now wrap the weaving wire around the central wire.

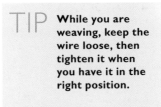

TIP **While you are weaving, keep the wire loose, then tighten it when you have it in the right position.**

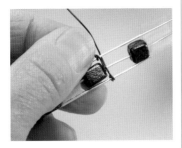

5 Take the weaving wire around the other outer wire, then bring it flat against the back of the bangle. Now go back to wrapping the first wire again, as in step 3.

6 Repeat the process to create a small woven section. Trim off any loose ends of wire and press the ends to make sure the work is smooth. Press the woven section together. Add more beads and woven sections as you fill the bracelet.

7 When you reach the end of each side and the end of the central wire, change to flat-wrapping between the two outer wires.

8 Roll in the wires at the open end of your bangle to form loops. Add a double hook to this side, then finish by shaping the bangle around a mandrel or other tubular object.

Hoop earrings

You can make hoop earrings quickly and customize them in many different ways. There are two different types of hoop earrings: those that go through your ear and ones that hang from earwires, so it is fun to try both.

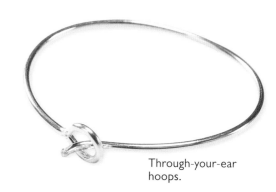

Through-your-ear hoops.

Through-your-ear hoops

For these earrings you will need to practice with basic wires, then switch to either sterling silver or gold wires to go through your ears once you are comfortable with your design.

TOOLS

1 Wire cutters
2 Mandrel or tubular object
3 Round-nose pliers
4 File or cup burr
5 Chain-nose pliers

1 For a very basic earring, work with 4 in. (10 cm) of 20 gauge (0.8 mm) wire in half-hard wire. First wrap the wire firmly round your mandrel to create the hoop shapes.

2 Using your round-nose pliers, make a 90-degree turn in one side of the wire about ½ in. (1 cm) from the end. Smooth the end of this wire with a file.

3 Holding your pliers horizontally, roll this wire around them to create a loop. Give your loop a small squeeze with your chain-nose pliers to flatten it.

4 Trim off any excess wire on the other side and flick up the end of the wire.

5 Smooth this end thoroughly with your file or cup burr.

TIP **Hammering these earrings would make them look more special and would work-harden the metal.**

Beaded hoop earrings

You can vary these earrings by adding beads to them and creating a hinge to keep the beads in place.

1 Start as on page 102, making a loop at one end of the wire. Thread beads onto the wire.

2 Once you have added all your beads to the wire, roll the other end of the wire to create a hinge. You can smooth it with your chain-nose pliers.

3 Straighten this wire and work out the length that you will need to go through your ears. Trim off the surplus wire. Flick up the end as you did with the simple hoops. Smooth the end of the wire with the file.

Dangly hoop earrings.

Hoop earrings on earwires

This is an even more dangly version of hoop earrings that hang from earwires. You can use any wires for these earrings as the hoops won't go through your ears.

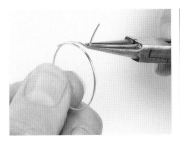

1 Cut your wire and wind it round the tubular object as before. Using your round-nose pliers, turn ½ in. (1 cm) at the end of the wire. This time turn it upward. Add beads to your wire if you would like to.

2 Repeat on the other side of the wire. Then roll both ends of the wire in opposite directions to create upward-facing loops.

3 Use a jump ring that you have made (see page 29) or a bought jump ring to link your two loops together.

4 Finally, add an earwire.

Brooches

You can use wires in many different ways to create a range of different brooches. A few techniques for different designs are offered here. Once you have conquered the fundamentals, you will be able to adapt the techniques to produce your own designs.

A brooch made from electrical wire that has been glued onto the brooch back and then reshaped.

Working with brooch pins

You can have a great time using ready-made brooch backs and decorating them with many different arrangements of wire. You can use the decorative shapes on pages 44–50, twisted wire stems as shown on page 89, wired buttons, or just scraps of recycled wire.

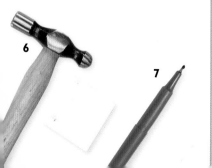

1. First make your decorations, using some of the decorative shapes. You will need about 10 in. (25 cm) of fairly heavy-gauge wire to make each stem. Coil up the end of the stem with chain- or wide-nose pliers.

2. To bind the decorations onto your brooch pin, you will need about 20 in. (50 cm) of a lighter-gauge wire. Open the pin, arrange the stems against it and start wrapping in the center of the pin. Allow plenty of wire on either side.

3. Wrap in both directions as tightly as you can until you have filled the brooch pin.

4. Trim off the ends of your wires and press them into the back of the brooch pin.

5. Now that you have everything in place, you can arrange the tops of the stems as you want them. You can also coil the bottoms of the stems some more if necessary.

Decorative shapes brooch.

Simple free-form brooch with wrapped beads.

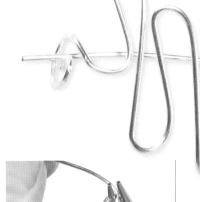
Plain wire free-form brooch.

Free-form brooch

You can have great fun making free-form brooches. They can be simple or elaborate—just let your creativity flow.

I You will need a heavy-gauge wire and your heavier tools for these pins. Try working with 10 in. (25 cm) of 16 gauge (1.25 mm) soft wire. Cut and file one end to make it neat. Then make a gentle curl in it.

2 Start to bend your wire into a decorative shape. Remember that you will need to end up opposite your first curl, with enough wire to make a loop and a pin. You can add beads or wrapping wires as you form your shape.

3 Roll your wire around the tip of your round-nose pliers at the other end of your shape to create a complete loop.

4 Now use your pliers down the straight length of wire to strengthen your pin; trim the end if necessary and file it. Using your wide- or chain-nose pliers, gently bend in the first coil so that it will hold the pin efficiently.

TIP **Think about how you want to wear your brooch. You will need to file the pin to a sharp point if you want it to go through fabrics, but a smoothly rounded end will work well on jumpers.**

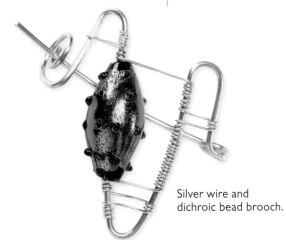

Silver wire and dichroic bead brooch.

Coil brooch

A coil pin or brooch is a little more complex than the free-form type, but can produce some attractive results. It can be used plain or decorated. You can experiment with different gauges of wire and try for a neat coil or a more free-form one.

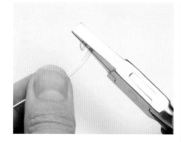

Start with 15 in. (38 cm) of 20 gauge (0.8 mm) wire. Bend the wire in half and start to form the double coil shown on page 45.

2 Stop forming your coil when you have about 3 ½ in. (9 cm) of straight wire remaining on each end of the wire. Pressing your chain-nose pliers against the edge of the coil, flick out your outer wire at a right angle.

18 gauge (1.0 mm) wire brooch with pearl decoration.

Plain 20 gauge (0.8 mm) wire coil brooch.

3 You can hammer your coil if you want to, then bend the angle that you have just made so that the wire is facing away from the coil. Work the other length of wire around to the opposite side of the coil.

4 Now place your round-nose pliers against the angled wire and roll it around them to make a complete loop next to the coil. Your wire will end up running across the back of your coil. Work-harden it with your fingers or pliers. You have now created the pin for your brooch. Trim the end of the pin and file the end.

Bend the wire at the other side of your coil so that this is also facing inward.

6 Now place your round-nose pliers against this wire and form the curve that will hold your pin. Trim off the end of this wire and turn in the end.

TIP **You can make a stronger brooch if you use 18 gauge (1.0 mm) wire. You are unlikely to be able to make a neat coil with this weight of wire but you should achieve an attractive, fluid shape.**

Kilt pin brooch

By adding a few beads and wrapping wires to your own kilt pin, you can create a decorative piece of jewelry without much effort.

Decorated kilt pin.

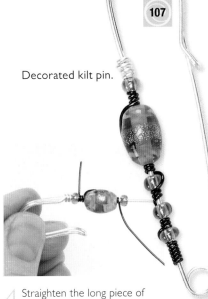

1 For this pin, you will need 12 in. (30 cm) of 18 gauge (1 mm) wire. Start by running your fingers or pliers down to the end of the wire to smooth it out. Now fold over about 4 in. (10 cm) with your round-nose pliers.

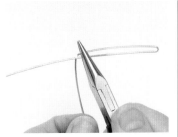

2 Put your chain-nose pliers across the folded wire about 2 in. (5 cm) from the shorter end and wind this end back around the longer wire.

3 Fold the doubled end over a fairly wide pen or similar tubular object. Then flick out the end of the wire with your pliers.

4 Straighten the long piece of wire again, then decorate it with beads and wraps of wire.

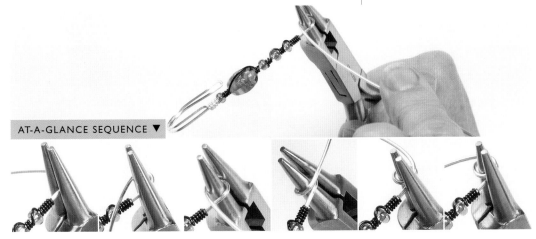

AT-A-GLANCE SEQUENCE ▼

5 Use the widest part of your large round-nose pliers to form a double loop next to the beads and wraps.

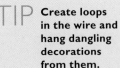

6 To finish the kilt pin, straighten the last length of wire and trim off the end so that it tucks neatly into your folded end. File the end so that it is smooth enough to go through garments.

TIP **Create loops in the wire and hang dangling decorations from them.**

Rings

Traditionally, rings are made using silversmithing techniques, but you can certainly have success with wire techniques too. Three techniques are shown in this section. When you have mastered them, adapt them to create other designs of your own.

Plain wire spiral ring.

Spiral ring

This is a quick way to make an adjustable ring.

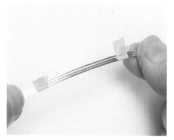

1 Cut three lengths of 18 gauge (1 mm) wire about 5 ½ in. (14 cm) long. Straighten them a little so that they are easy to handle. Use masking tape to hold them firmly together in the middle, but leave spaces for your wrapping wire.

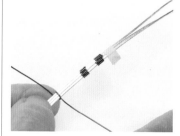

2 Now cut some lengths of a fine gauge wire and use it to wrap the center of your wires, in one place or in little groups. Trim off the wrapping wire neatly.

3 Now curve the wires completely around the mandrel or tubular object.

4 Find the center of your ring and position your wrappings as you want them, then press them firmly. Remove the masking tape.

5 Gently spread out the ends of your wires. One by one, trim them to the length that you want, file the ends, and then roll them back.

TOOLS

1 Wire cutters
2 Masking tape
3 Mandrel or tubular object, roughly the size of the knuckle on your ring finger
4 Chain- or wide-nose pliers
5 Round-nose pliers
6 File or cup burr

6

TIP **You could use this design on a much larger scale to make a bangle.**

Bead ring

Now you can try making a ring that uses a bead as a centerpiece. Choose a strong bead and one that won't be too wide against your finger.

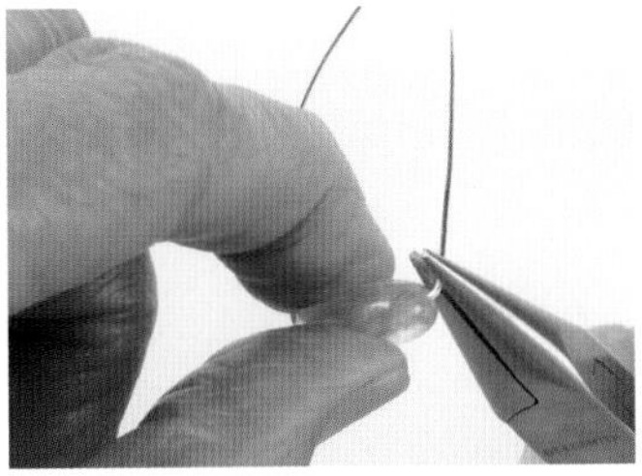

1 Start by making the shaft for your ring. The technique shown here uses a stone bead about ½ in. (1 cm) wide and 10 in. (25 cm) of 20 gauge (0.8 mm) wire. Place the bead in the center of the wire and fold the wire back with your chain-nose pliers.

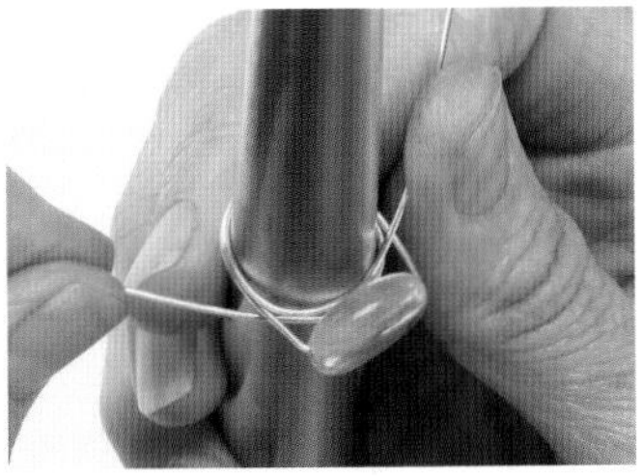

2 Now work your wire round a mandrel or a tubular object. You will bring it right round and under the bead so that the ring has a double shaft and there are two wires running under the bead.

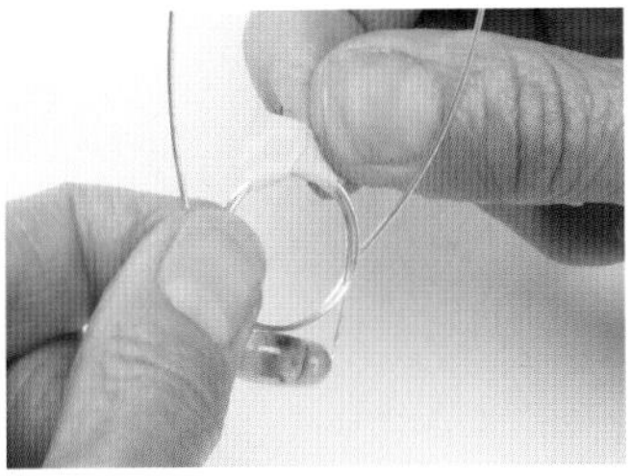

3 Use a piece of masking tape to hold the shaft firmly in place.

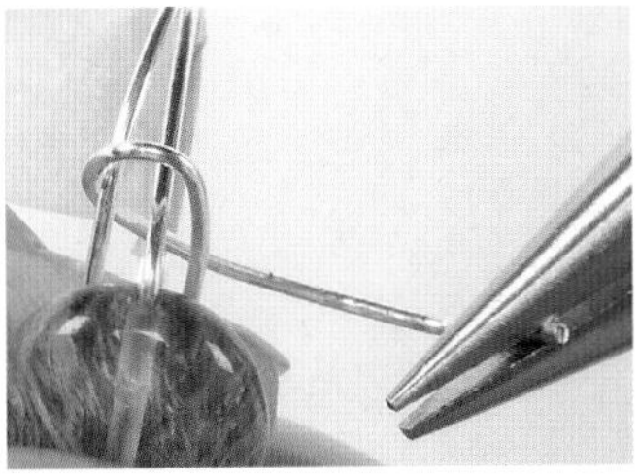

4 Holding all the parts firmly together under the bead, use your chain-nose pliers to wind the wire back down the shaft. You will need to keep the wraps wide as you work so that the wire doesn't kink. Wrap about three times, then trim off the end of the wire and press the end in with your pliers.

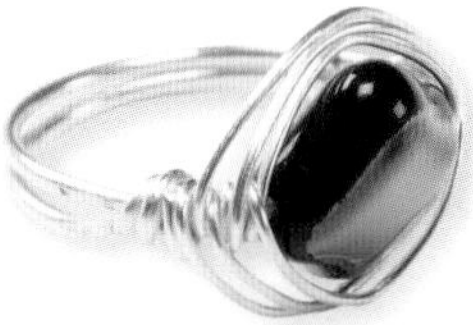

Dichroic bead ring with herringbone wrap.

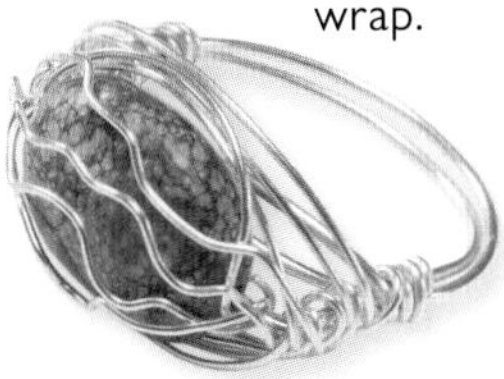

Russian serpentine ring with wrapping pulled over the top.

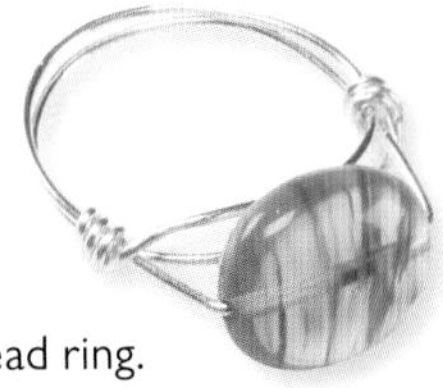

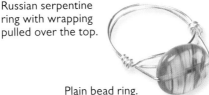

Plain bead ring.

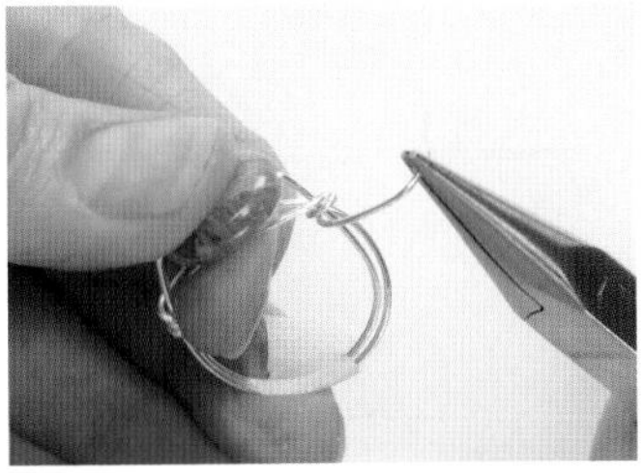

5 Repeat the process on the other side of the ring. You now have a basic bead ring.

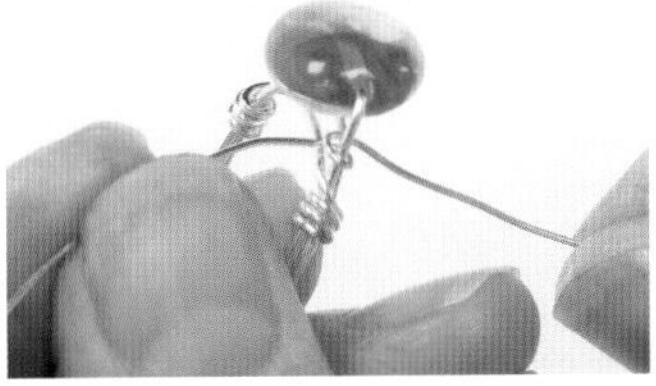

6 If wished, you can wrap another wire beneath your bead. Attach a length, about 20 in. (50 cm) long, of fine-gauge wire beneath the bead, leaving a tail so that you have some control. Either just make plain wraps below the bead, or try using the herringbone wrap on page 72.

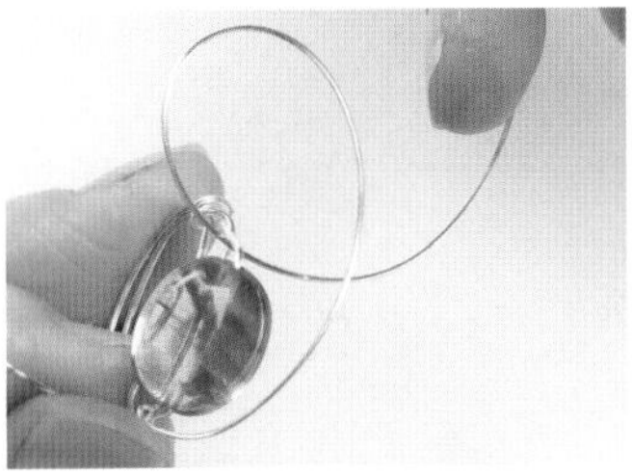

7 Take the wire around to the back of the shaft on the other side of your ring and work it around to the front. Now take it round the back and wrap from the front to the back on that side. Now that the wire is secure, trim off the tail. Repeat the process on the other side of the bead, pulling out the wire to create an elegant pattern. When you have filled the space, you can finish off.

TIP **When you have practiced making a ring like this, try making the shaft with a thicker wire, as thick a gauge as you can get through your bead. It will be harder to work but will give a better result. If you have to work with thinner wires, you can always bind the shaft as shown on the Cluster bead ring (see page 110).**

Cluster bead ring

This ring looks complicated but is only a little more difficult to make than the bead ring on the previous page.

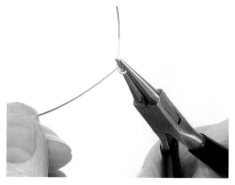

1 Start by threading a selection of beads onto headpins ready to make the clusters. You will probably need to reduce the length of the headpins to make a neat single loop under each bead.

2 Now start to make your ring, using 10 in. (25 cm) of 20 gauge (0.8 mm) wire. With your round-nose pliers, form a loop in the center of the wire.

TIP **You could experiment with making more loops in the shaft of your ring to make the cluster more dense. Or you could wire lots of tiny beads onto the loops with very fine wires to create a different look.**

3 Now make another loop on either side of the central one. Flatten them all with your chain-nose pliers so that they sit neatly next to each other.

4 Measure your finger and add a little extra length as your ring shaft will be wrapped. Find the position on the mandrel or tubular object that corresponds to this length. Now wrap your wire round the mandrel at this point. You need to wrap around so that your wire goes across the top of the ring three times, as you did with the bead ring on page 109.

5 Secure the bottom of the ring with masking tape, then wind the remaining wire down on either side away from the center of the ring, again as you did in the bead ring. Trim off the ends and smooth them into the shaft with your wide-nose pliers.

6 Add the cluster beads to the loops at the top of your ring. You will open their loops sideways and work them into the loops on the ring, closing them again securely. Work on as many pieces of the cluster as will fit comfortably.

7 Finally remove the tape from the bottom of the ring and bind the shaft in with a fine gauge wire, pushing the end of this new wire in place with your chain-nose pliers.

Amethyst chip and bead cluster ring.

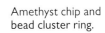

Filled shapes

Other pages in this book offer numerous suggestions for ways to combine beads and wire to create pendants, bracelets, and earrings. An additional technique is to form a shape in wire that you can then fill with wire and beads. It is a good idea to start with a pendant, as earrings are harder if you want them to match.

Pearl pendant.

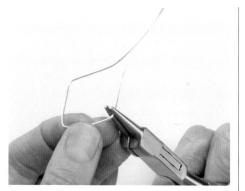

1 Cut some heavy-gauge wire, such as 18 gauge (1.0 mm) to create a frame for your pendant. You can make your shape either by wrapping it round a circular shape, free-form, or by using a jig as shown on page 53.

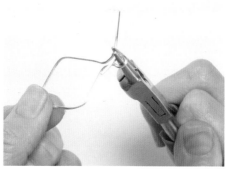

2 Make two loops facing in different directions at the top of your shape. If you hammer the shape now you will find it easier to handle.

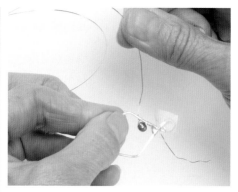

3 Use some masking tape to hold the two loops together, then start wrapping the top of your shape so that the two loops are held firmly together. Use a fine-gauge wire to do this. Now start to fill up your shape. Wind your wire down the outside, then thread on a bead and wrap the wire around the outside again.

TOOLS

1 Wire cutters

2 Round-nose pliers

3 Hammer and block (optional)

4 Masking tape

5 Acrylic-nose pliers (optional)

6 Jig (see page 114)

7 Gizmo (see page 114)

8 Chain-nose pliers (see page 117)

6

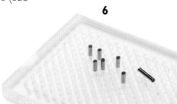

Mixed semi-precious bead pendant with added wire spirals.

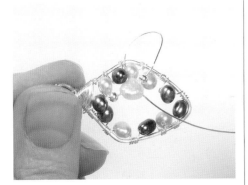

4 Continue to work around the outside of the shape, adding beads at the edges. When you have filled the edges, start to run wires across the shape to fill the center.

5 Aim to fill the shape as completely as you can, as neatly or messily as you like. You can add more wire as you add your beads. Finish off on one side of the frame. Use your acrylic-nose pliers to smooth your wire if it becomes kinked as you work.

6 Add a closed-loop section to your top loops so that you can hang this piece as a pendant.

TIP **Use this technique to create elaborate cuff bracelets by making a frame, then filling it with beads as shown here.**

Butterfly pendant

As well as making pendants or bangles out of geometric shapes, try using this method of creating a framework filled with wire and beads for more sculptural forms. This butterfly, made using a jig, is one design you could try, or you could experiment with other figurative or abstract shapes.

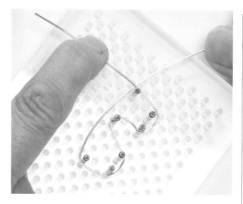

1 Create a shape that you like with your jig, positioning the pegs and using scraps of wire to make the outline. For this butterfly, make two copies of the shape in heavier wire, such as 15 in. (38 mm) of 20 gauge (0.8 mm) wire. The two shapes will form the two matching halves of the butterfly.

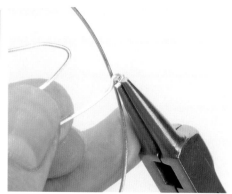

2 Working on one half at a time, trim off the shorter end of the wire and roll it with your round-nose pliers so that you can catch the other side of the wire. Leave it open at this point.

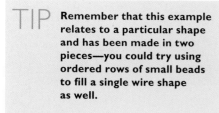

TIP **Remember that this example relates to a particular shape and has been made in two pieces—you could try using ordered rows of small beads to fill a single wire shape as well.**

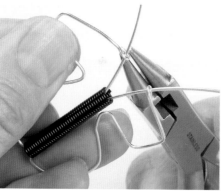

3 Now create a center to join the two halves of the butterfly together, such as this Gizmo spiral, made on the wider of the winders (see page 91). Run the long wires of the two halves up through the spiral. Then close the loops. Alternatively, you could use a bead with a very wide hole.

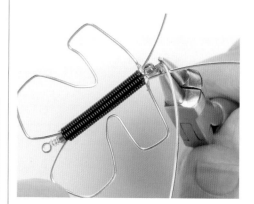

4 Take another wire through the center of the spiral and make a closed loop at the top of it. You can add a couple of beads if you like. The pendant will hang from this top loop. You will have to pull everything out of shape while you do this, then rearrange it.

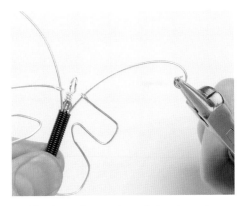

5 The long wires can be coiled at the ends to form the antennae of the butterfly.

Beaded butterfly pendant.

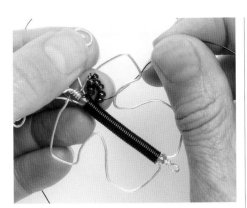

6 Now start to fill the shape, using a very fine-gauge wire such as 28 gauge (0.3 mm). Wind it around the structure to start off, then begin to add beads.

7 Continue until you have completely filled the structure, following a random or more regular design.

8 If you wish, you can add more beads as an edging to the shape.

Simple wire tiara

There are many different ideas for tiara designs. If you want to make one, you can use the previous two techniques. Also look at the decorative shapes on pages 44–50 to see which of these you could use. This example here uses simple wire structures to create the tiara.

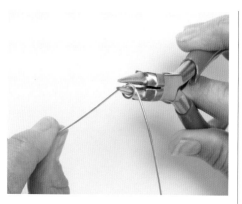

1 You will need a basic tiara frame, available from an online supplier or a bead store, on which to build your structure. For this structure, use 18 in. (46 cm) of 18 gauge (1.0 mm) wire. With your round-nose pliers, form a complete loop in the center of the wire. Then bring both sides of the wire down toward the tiara frame. Straighten the sides with your fingers.

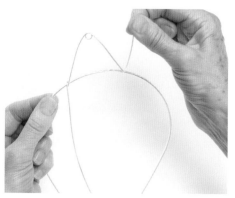

2 Position this structure against the frame and wind the wire round the frame a couple of times on each side.

> TIP **The ideas here are intended to inspire you to think of other designs. This is a very simple tiara—you could make one with many more shapes standing up from the tiara frame, by using gold and silver wires together, or by completely filling the structures.**

3 Move your pliers to one side of the wire and roll it around them to create another downward-facing loop. Mark the position on the wire and recreate a matching loop in the same place on the other side.

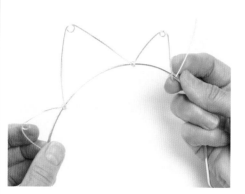

4 Attach both sides to the frame to complete the basic structure.

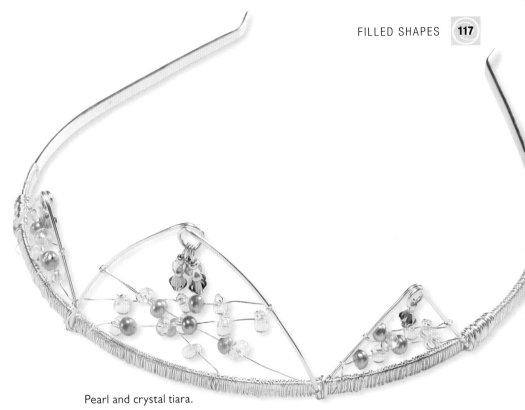

5 Now for the fun bit—decorating your tiara. You can make small hanging pieces, using headpins or eyepins, to dangle from the top loops.

Pearl and crystal tiara.

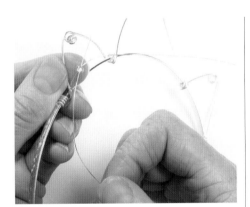

6 Fill in the structure of your tiara as much as you like. If preferred, you can keep it simple with just a few strands of decoration as here, with 28 gauge (0.3 mm) wire crisscrossing into the outline of the tiara.

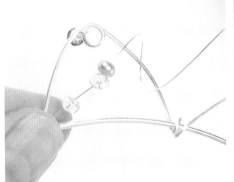

7 You can fix beads into place by threading back through them as shown on page 95. The pearls here have very small holes, so they are left loose.

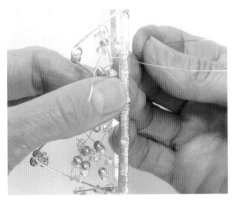

8 When you are happy with your decoration, it's a good idea to use more of the fine wire to wrap the tiara frame and make it look more finished. Trim off any loose ends of wire and use your chain-nose pliers to smooth the ends into the structure.

CHAPTER TWO
Toward Silversmithing

The final section of the book is designed to bridge the gap between wirework and metalwork, by giving you an insight into some basic silversmithing techniques. You will need more equipment to practice these skills, but the techniques have been demonstrated with the simplest tools available.

Tools for silver wirework

Tools and wires have been discussed in general at the beginning of the book (see page 8). The tools and wires described here can be used in other ways but are also relevant to this section of the book.

Different types and shapes of silver wire

The two main types of silver available from bullion companies are sterling silver (925), which is most commonly used in jewelry manufacture; and fine silver (999), which is pure silver. The numbers in brackets indicate the percentage of silver contained in that type—92.5 percent and 99.9 percent—the rest being made up from other metals. Fine silver is much softer because it has a higher silver content.

The different shapes of silver wire available will vary according to your supplier, but generally you should be able to buy round, square, oval, D-shaped, rectangular, and bearer, which is used for stone setting.

Round, D-shaped, and rectangular wire come in a large range of sizes and diameters, from 0.2 mm up to 9.5 mm diameter for round wire. D-shaped and rectangular wire is mainly used for making rings or bangles.

Thicker wire may need to be annealed to make it easier to bend (see page 122). The purpose of annealing is to soften the silver and make it more pliable and easier to bend. If you are going to draw down wire through a draw plate, you will also need to anneal silver to change its shape.

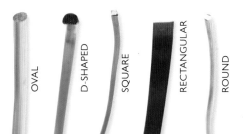

OVAL D-SHAPED SQUARE RECTANGULAR ROUND

Soldering tools

These are the basic tools you will need to solder or fuse and melt silver.

⌃ TORCH
There are a variety of different torches available. Professional-grade torches are useful if you are doing a lot of soldering, or you can buy butane/propane mix torches with replaceable canisters in DIY stores. Alternatively you could use small-scale catering torches that are refilled with butane lighter fuel; however, these are only suitable for small-scale soldering projects.

⌃ HEATPROOF MAT
Mats are available as asbestos substitute sheets or blocks. You could also use a fire brick or charcoal block, but you must make sure it is suitable to cope with the heat.

⌃ SAFETY PICKLE
This is a powdered mild acid that is mixed with water and kept warm in a slow cooker with a ceramic inner pot. Soldered or annealed pieces of silver are placed into it to clean them.

⌃ TWEEZERS
You will need one pair of stainless steel tweezers for dealing with solder (bottom), and one pair of plastic or brass tweezers to use in the safety pickle (middle). Reverse-action tweezers, which open when squeezed (top), are also useful.

⌃ SILVER SOLDER
Silver solders are available in varying widths. They come in the form of strips of silver that indicate the temperature at which each solder melts. The different grades are: enameling, hard, medium, easy, and extra-easy. Silver solder is also available in wire or syringe form.

⌃ FLUX
This is painted with a small paintbrush onto the join to be soldered. It keeps the silver clean from oxides in the metal. The most common product is borax, which is available as a powder or solid cone.

⌃ SNIPS
You can use either tin snips or side cutters to cut the strips of solder into small pieces (pallions).

Other tools

Below is a selection of other useful silversmithing tools.

‹ MANDREL
A mandrel is a tapered steel or wooden former that is used to shape metal. Mandrels can be round, oval, square, teardrop, or hexagonal in cross-section; the one shown here is a ring mandrel.

⌃ MALLET
A leather rawhide, wooden, or plastic mallet is used to hammer metal without leaving a mark. A mallet is usually used to shape metal without stretching it.

⌃ RING CLAMP
Wooden hand-held clamps with leather pads are used to hold rings safely, without damaging their shanks, for decorating.

⌃ FLAT STEEL BLOCK OR PLATE
The flat surface of a steel block is useful for flattening sheet and wire, or to support work as it is forged, riveted, or textured with punches or hammers.

‹ FLAT FILES
Used for work on flat surfaces, such as filing between joins to be soldered, edges, and outside curves. The flat needle file (left) is used for more detailed work than the flat file (far left).

‹ FLAT-ENDED HAMMER
A flat-ended hammer can be used for all heavy work. It can forge out lumps of molten silver, give a heavy texture on metal, and be used for reshaping.

‹ POLISHING WHEEL
A polishing wheel is an electric motor with a horizontal shaft. Polishing mops and brushes can be screwed onto the shaft and polish or liquid soap applied to them. The workspace should be ventilated because the polish can be rather dirty and create a lot of dust.

⌃ CENTER PUNCH
A center punch is a little metal tool, similar in shape and size to a pencil. One end has a point and the other is blunt and flat. The point is positioned on the metal where a hole is to be drilled. The blunt end is struck with a hammer.

⌃ DRAW PLATE AND TONGS
Draw plates are used to reduce the diameter of wire or to produce a different profile, such as triangular, square, and oval. This is done by annealing the wire and drawing it through the appropriate hole in the draw plate (see page 123).

‹ VISE
There are two types of bench vise. One is quite small, able to turn in all directions and has "safe" or plastic jaws. The other is a more heavy-duty vise, which is used to hold stakes, mandrels, and draw plates. Ideally, both types should be fixed permanently to the bench.

Basic skills

This section will help to develop your wirework techniques and increase the range of skills to use in your projects.

Annealing silver

The purpose of annealing silver is to make it softer and easier to shape. You will be making all the molecules in the silver lie in the same direction, which is why it becomes softer and easier to bend. Cooling it down doesn't harden it as it would with some other metals.

1 Lay the piece of wire to be annealed on the heatproof mat.

2 Light the torch to a medium flame and heat the wire evenly, trying not to concentrate on any one area. Be careful not to overheat the silver and melt it, but heat the whole piece evenly until it becomes a dull red. When it is this color all over, turn off the torch.

3 Pick up the wire with steel tweezers and place it in the pickle to clean it.

4 Leave the wire until it is clean, then remove it with the brass tweezers, and rinse and dry.

5 This is how your wire looks before and after it has been pickled.

TIP **ALWAYS remember to use brass tweezers when you remove the silver from the pickle. If your steel tweezers make contact with the pickle they will copper plate the silver and turn the pickle green.**

Drawing down wire

The purpose of drawing down wire is to change the profile and diameter of the wire. This gives you the scope to change your own wire if you run out of a particular gauge. You need a specialist piece of equipment called a draw plate and tongs for this process.

Many different draw plates are available. They take the form of flat pieces of steel with different sizes of holes drilled into them. You can get varying diameters of round holes used to reduce the diameter of round wire. Or you can get differently shaped holes, such as square and triangular, which you can use to change the profile of a wire.

1 You must first anneal the wire to be drawn down. If annealing very thin wire, wrap it into a coil and avoid having any ends protruding, then anneal the wire as before. Make sure it is pickled, rinsed, and completely dry, otherwise it will rust the draw plate.

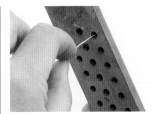

2 File a point on the wire and try pushing it into the holes of the draw plate until you find one that the wire will just go through. Push through from the side with indents at the back of the holes—the other side of the plate is completely smooth.

3 Clamp the draw plate in the vise. Holding the pointed end of the wire with the tongs, pull it slowly right through the hole to reduce or change its shape. Repeat until you get to the size or shape that you require. Remember to anneal again after three or four passes.

Hammering and forging wire

Hammering and forging are further ways of changing the profile and shape of wire or metal. They can be used to create decorative metal surfaces or to change the shape of a wire. When hammering silver, remember that the more you hammer, the harder and more brittle it will become, so you will need to anneal it again to make it pliant.

Planished effect with round-ended hammer.

Ridge effect with cross pein hammer.

TEXTURING WITH HAMMERS
Planishing and chasing (indenting marks and patterns into metal) are traditional silversmithing techniques, but they can be successfully used as a decorative surface pattern on silver wire jewelry projects. The shape of the end of the hammer or tool will dictate the type of mark you make. A popular finish, which can also be called planishing, is created by using a round-ended hammer to produce a dimpled finish and a shimmering effect when polished.

1 First anneal the silver that you are using (see opposite). A 2 in. (5 cm) rectangular silver wire is shown here. To planish the piece of wire or rod, place it on the flat steel block.

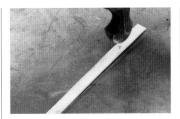

2 Using a round-ended steel hammer, such as this embossing or chasing hammer, hit the surface of the silver. Work evenly over the surface, ideally overlapping each hammer mark over the one before, so that there are no flat areas left.

3 Try using different-shaped hammers to create different surface patterns on the silver. A cross pein raising hammer, that has a ridge on the end, produces long ridges on the silver.

FORGING

Basic forging consists of hammering the silver with a flat-ended steel hammer onto a flat steel base or stake, in order to stretch the silver in different directions while at the same time thinning it. This can be a useful technique with wire or rod when you want to taper the ends without filing away any silver.

1 Try forging a 2 mm square silver rod to taper the ends to make a bangle. First anneal the silver rod along its whole length on the heatproof mat. After annealing, pickle the rod until it is clean, then remove it from the pickle using the brass tweezers, rinse, and dry.

2 Hold the rod flat against the steel block, about a third of the way along the rod from the end. Using a flat-ended hammer, strike the rod and keep turning it through one rotation, while continuing to hit it with the hammer.

AT-A-GLANCE SEQUENCE ▼

3 After going all the way around one section of the rod, start striking it slightly lower down, repeating the process until you have worked down the whole length—this will stretch the rod and thin it. Now concentrate your hammering further and further down the rod until it starts to taper evenly all the way down. As the rod starts to toughen up, remember to anneal it occasionally. When finished, you can either leave the hammer marks or file the tapered end and sand it smooth.

4 Use the rod in a design of your choice—here it has been used as part of a bangle. Remember that the forging process stretches the rod, so you need to allow for that extra length in your measurements.

TIP **You don't have to use traditional, specialist tools to make textures on silver. Try working with household objects, such as the end of a screwdriver, or use a household hammer to hit the end.**

Try and avoid hitting the steel block with the hammer when you are forging as this can ruin both.

Melting wire ends

Once you know how to anneal wire, you can begin some simple techniques that involve heating it. In this example, melting the end of the wire produces a bobble-shaped finial that can stop wire from coming out of a hole, or stop a bead from sliding off the wire. Use it to create a smooth end on a piece of wire, or to link pieces of silver.

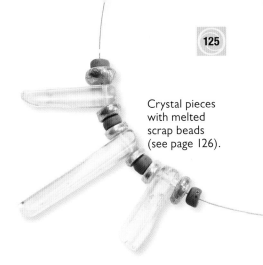

Crystal pieces with melted scrap beads (see page 126).

Making headpins

You can use headpins for creating earrings, earwires, or drops for pendants.

1 Cut two pieces of 20 gauge (0.8 mm) round silver wire, at least 3 in. (7 cm) long. Hold one wire with steel or reverse-action tweezers over the heatproof mat, with one end of the wire hanging down toward it. Using the hottest part of a medium flame (the end of the dark blue area), heat the wire with the torch.

2 When the end of the wire glows red, it will start to melt and a bobble will appear that creeps up the wire. The size of bobble depends on how much you melt the wire—the trick is to match the bobbles on both wires. Practice this technique to get used to the heat at which the wire melts.

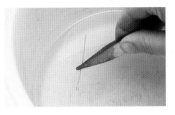

3 Transfer the wire to the pickle to clean it. Leave for about five minutes or until it is clean, then remove it with brass or plastic tweezers. Repeat the process for the second piece of wire.

4 With a flat file, file the other end of the wire and sand it smooth.

5 To polish the wires, you could either wire brush them or put them into a barrel polisher. They are now ready to use as head pins for beads.

TOOLS

1 Snips
2 Steel tweezers (reverse-action if you have them)
3 Heatproof mat
4 Torch
5 Pickle
6 Brass or plastic tweezers
7 Flat file
8 Sandpaper

9 Brass wire brush or barrel polisher
10 Tubular object (see page 126)
11 Round-nose pliers (see page 126)
12 Flat steel block (see page 126)
13 Flat-ended hammer (see page 126)
14 Center punch (see page 126)
15 Drill (see page 126)

1

Fused wire loops

Fusing involves melting the surface of the silver so that when two melted surfaces touch they will join, without solder or flux. These fused loops work well as links in chains or as part of a toggle clasp. Because the silver has been melted, it has an attractive rough texture.

Pendants and chains using fused loops.

1 | Using 20 gauge (0.8 mm) sterling wire, wrap it around a tubular object of the right size, at least 5 or 6 times. Snip off the excess wire and slide the coils off. Use the round-nose pliers to tuck the ends neatly into the loop.

2 | Put the coils of wire on the heatproof mat and light the torch. Heat the coils until they glow red and begin to melt. Be careful not to overheat the wire as it will completely melt.

3 | When you are pleased with the effect and the wire is joined, pick up the loop with steel tweezers and transfer to the pickle to clean. Leave for about 5 minutes, remove with the brass tweezers, rinse, and dry.

4 | To polish the loop, you can use a soft brass bristle brush which creates a satiny look on the silver—brush across the loop on both sides. If you have one available, a barrel polisher will give a shinier finish.

Melted-down scrap beads

This is a good way to use up leftover scraps of silver wire. Be careful to keep your silver plate wire and silver wire separate: the silver plate cannot be melted down in the same way as it has a copper core.

> **TIP** To make it safer to drill the hole, put the bead into a clamp so that your fingers aren't too close to the drill bit.

AT-A-GLANCE SEQUENCE ▼

1 | Place a pile of your scrap pieces of wire onto the heatproof mat or charcoal block. Turn on the torch, bring it to a high flame, and point it at the silver, using the hottest part—the end of the blue part of the flame. Heat the silver until it goes bright red and starts to melt. The scraps will ball up and shrink together. You can tell when the silver is completely molten: it will start to spin and will produce a small ball. This will be flattened on the mat side.

2 | Pick up the ball with the steel tweezers, put it in the pickle to clean, then remove it with brass or plastic tweezers. Wash and dry the ball, then put it, with the flattened side down, onto a flat steel block or surface. Using a flat-ended hammer, hammer the ball on the other side to flatten it. Place the point of a center punch in the middle of the ball and hit it with a hammer to make an indent.

3 | Insert a drill bit made for metal into the drill—it should be the appropriate size for the material you will thread with. Place some wood under the bead, put the bit into the indent, and, holding the drill at 90 degrees to the bead, drill through it. Sand around the hole and polish the bead with a brass brush for a satin finish, or a barrel polisher for a high shine. Repeat to make as many beads as you like.

Silver soldering

Another important addition to your skills is to learn how to solder pieces of wire together so that you can start to create rings or solid jump rings. You will also use these techniques to decorate with wire.

TIP **There are five grades of silver solder (see page 120). The grade you use will depend on how many times you are going to solder on the same piece of silver. As you only solder the jump ring once, you can use any grade of solder.**

Soldering jump rings

Start by soldering jump rings as a way of learning basic soldering techniques.

To solder up a jump ring, take two pairs of wide-nose pliers and tightly close the sterling silver jump ring so that both sides are touching. Place the jump ring on the heatproof mat.

Now get some flux ready. Put a little water into the borax dish and move the borax cone around in the dish to make the borax dissolve. The liquid should look like thin cream.

Paint the flux onto the join of the jump ring—this will prevent oxidization of the metal, letting the solder flow and join the silver together.

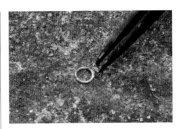

Using the snips, cut a very small piece of solder (pallion). Using the steel tweezers, dip the pallion into the borax and place it onto the join of the ring.

TOOLS

1 Two pairs of wide-nose pliers

2 Heatproof mat

3 Flux (borax)

4 Paintbrush

5 Snips

6 Silver solder

7 Steel tweezers

8 Torch

9 Pickle

10 Brass or plastic tweezers

11 Flat file

12 Sandpaper

Have the torch at a low flame—the small jump ring will heat up very quickly. Heat the whole ring evenly and don't get one side of the join hotter than the other because the solder will attach to the hottest area. When the silver gets to the temperature at which solder melts, it will flow into the join and solder it together.

Pick up the jump ring with the tweezers and place it in the pickle, making sure the tweezers do not touch the pickle or they will contaminate it. Leave the ring in the pickle until it has removed the black oxides and the flux. The jump ring will look white when it is clean. Remove it with brass or plastic tweezers, wash and dry.

You can file away any excess solder left on the join, then sand it to remove any file marks. The ring is now ready to polish and use.

Making chains

A chain can be as simple or as complicated as you like. The simplest chain is made from jump rings linked together and soldered. But you can vary the effect with techniques such as hammering, or using different profiles or sizes of wire.

Chain-making techniques

To familiarize yourself with the technique, start with a large hammered link chain, using round wire to make the jump rings or links. Calculating how much wire you need can be difficult: work out the diameter of each link that you are using and divide the length that you need by the diameter of the link. It is always best to buy and make more than you need to allow for any mistakes or a change of the finished length.

Syringe solder is used here, but you could also use the soldering techniques shown on page 127.

1 Start by making the jump rings with 18–12 gauge (1–2 mm) silver round wire. Wrap the wire tightly around the tubular object. Wind it around as many times as you want links, plus a couple more times in case of mistakes.

2 Remove the loop from the tubing: you will now have a coil of wire. Using snips, cut through the coil in the same position all the way along to produce individual jump rings. If you are working with thicker wire you will need to cut with a piercing saw.

3 File each end of the jump ring flat, using a flat needle file.

TOOLS

1 Tubular object
2 Snips
3 Flat needle file
4 Two pairs of wide-nose pliers
5 Heatproof mat
6 Flux
7 Syringe silver
8 Torch
9 Pickle
10 Brass or plastic tweezers
11 Flat steel block or plate
12 Flat-ended steel hammer
13 Sandpaper
14 Reverse-action tweezers

4 Take half of your links and, using two pairs of wide-nose pliers, close up each one so that you have a good join. Place it on the heatproof mat and paint flux on to the join. Then add the syringe silver.

5 Light the torch and adjust to a medium flame. Heat the link evenly on both sides—if heated unevenly, the solder will attach to the hottest part and won't join the link. When the solder has run, drop the link into the pickle to clean for 5 minutes.

6 Remove the link from the pickle with brass tweezers, then wash and dry. Place on the steel flat block and, using a flat-ended hammer, hammer flat.

7 File and sand the join until you are sure it is smooth. Repeat the process with the remaining half of the links.

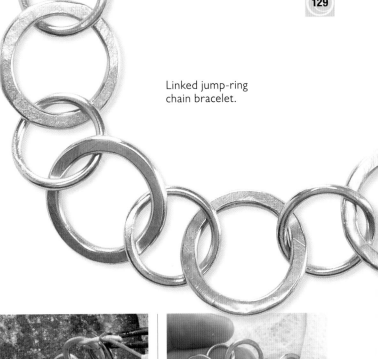

Linked jump-ring chain bracelet.

8 Using two pairs of wide-nose pliers, join up all the links, alternating one flattened link with one smooth link and ensuring that you have a good join on each one.

9 To solder the smooth links, paint flux just where they join.

10 Put the first link into the reverse-action tweezers with the join facing upward and add your solder. Light the torch and heat the link up evenly (the reverse-action tweezers take the heat away from the side they are attached to, which means you may need to heat that side more). Try not to heat the rest of the chain—angle your torch away from it as you work. Repeat with the other links that need to be soldered and then put the whole chain into the pickle to clean it.

11 Remove it from the pickle with brass tweezers, then wash and dry the chain. Check that all the links are properly soldered. If some are not, go back and repeat the process on the unsoldered ones. Use a flat file to file the joins until they cannot be seen, then sand them. To finish, polish the chain (see tip box at left).

TIP **Great care must be taken when polishing chains. Ideally it should be done in a barrel polisher which gives the chain a very shiny finish. If this isn't available, you could brush-polish the links with a large brass brush to give it a satin sheen, or polish each link individually on a polishing wheel. However, great care must be taken if using a wheel. Make sure you hold the rest of the links in your hands: if the wheel catches the chain, it might break it and possibly injure you. Always wear goggles and tie up your hair when polishing on a wheel.**

Making rings

Rings can be made with a variety of thicknesses and profiles of wire. It is very important to size the ring accurately.

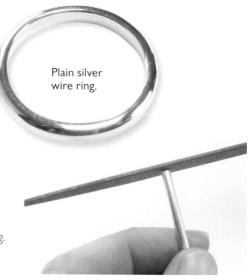

Plain silver wire ring.

Plain silver wire ring

Making a simple band ring is another excellent way to start to extend your metal working skills. Sterling silver wire can be bought in a large array of different shapes and sizes. A popular one for making rings is D-shaped wire, which looks like a traditional wedding-ring band. You will also need some specialist pieces of equipment for ring making. One is a mandrel, which is a tapered steel shape for bending and hammering the ring into shape. You will need a mallet too. This is made of rawhide so that you can hammer the silver into shape without indenting or marking it. To finish your ring, you will need polishing equipment.

Before you begin, work out the size of your ring. Calculate the length by adding a thickness and a half of the silver that you are using to the circumference of your finger. In this example, the silver wire is 2 mm thick, so you need to add on 3 mm to your finger size. With a flat needle file, file both ends of the silver to the length that you have calculated.

TIP **A simple low-tech way to size your finger is to use a strip of paper and wrap it around the widest part, usually your knuckle. It needs to be a very tight fit. Mark exactly where the paper overlaps.**

TOOLS

1 Flat needle file
2 Two pairs of wide-nose pliers
3 Flux
4 Heatproof mat
5 Snips
6 Medium solder
7 Torch
8 Steel tweezers
9 Pickle
10 Brass or plastic tweezers

11 Mandrel
12 Rawhide mallet
13 Half-round file
14 Sandpaper
15 Polishing attachments for drill, or polishing wheel and polish, or barrel polisher
16 Round-nose pliers (see page 132)
17 Easy solder (see page 132)
18 Reverse-action tweezers (see page 132)

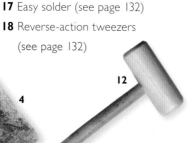

AT-A-GLANCE SEQUENCE ▼

2 Curve the wire with two pairs of wide-nose pliers to create a misshapen circle. If the wire is very thick, you may need to anneal it to make it more pliable. Bend the wire and get both ends to join tightly. It doesn't matter at this stage that the ring is not round. To get the two ends to join tightly it can help to push them past each other and bring them back in line so that they touch.

3 Paint flux onto the join and put the ring on the heatproof mat so it is lying flat on the surface. With the snips, cut a piece of medium solder. Dip it in the flux and place it on the join so that the solder is touching both sides of the join.

4 Adjust the torch to a medium flame and heat the whole ring. Make sure that neither side of the join gets hotter than the other, as the solder will attach to the hottest part and won't create the join. When the silver gets to the temperature at which the solder melts, the solder will run along the join and solder it together. With the steel tweezers, transfer the ring to the pickle and leave until clean. Remove with the brass or plastic tweezers, rinse, and dry.

5 Put the ring on the end of the mandrel and push it down as far as you can with your hands. Now take the mallet and hammer the ring down the mandrel as far as it will go. To make it completely round, you will need to twist the mandrel round as you hammer. If the ring gets stuck on the mandrel, turn it upside down and hit the ring with the mallet to knock it off. Try the ring on for size. If it is too small, you can stretch it slightly by hammering it further down the mandrel.

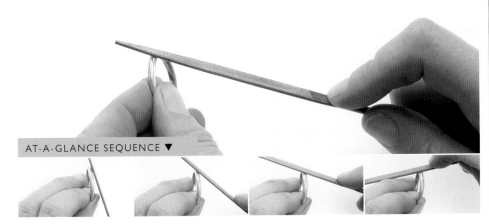

AT-A-GLANCE SEQUENCE ▼

6 Using the flat side of the half-round file, work the join until it disappears. Try to maintain the same profile as the shape of the wire so you don't thin the metal too much at the join. You can also file the join on the inside to make it disappear. Now use sandpaper to sand the join and remove the file marks for a smooth join.

7 There are several different methods that you can use to polish your ring. Try using small polishing attachments for drills with a little polish (tripoli or luster). Other options are to use a barrel polisher or polishing wheel.

Customizing ready-made silver rings

You can customize a ready-made silver band ring by soldering on pieces of shaped wire. You could use silver, copper, gold, or brass wire, all of which can be soldered onto silver. However, soldering on copper or brass means that a silver ring can not be hallmarked.

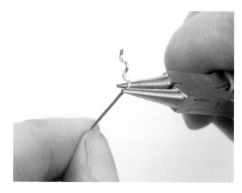

1 Using the round and wide-nose pliers, form a length of 20 gauge (0.8 mm) 9ct yellow gold round wire into a shape that will fit inside the width of the ring band. Cut it to length with the snips and file each end.

2 With a mandrel and rawhide mallet or your pliers, adjust the wire to match the outside circumference of the ring. You want it to sit comfortably on the ring and touch the band all the way along so that you can get a good soldered join.

3 Paint flux on the area of the ring to which the wire is to be soldered. Also paint it on the wire.

TIP **You can add different shapes, such as spirals of melted bobbles, to different profile rings.**

4 Hold the ring in the reverse-action tweezers so it is sitting on the heatproof mat. With the area to be soldered facing upward, place the wire on the ring.

5 Cut some small pieces of easy solder (pallion), dip them into the flux, and place them alongside the wire, so that the solder is touching both the ring and the wire. The smaller the pieces the better.

6 Adjust the torch to a medium flame—it is important that you heat the whole ring and not concentrate just on the area to be soldered. The solder will attach to the hottest part, so you must avoid the top area and mainly heat the band. As this heats up, move up to where the wire is. When the metal gets to the temperature at which the solder melts, it will flow along the wire and solder it onto the ring. If certain areas don't solder you can always pickle and redo the process.

7 With the steel tweezers, transfer the ring to the pickle to clean it. Then remove it with the brass or plastic tweezers and rinse and dry. Sand the top of the wire, removing any excess solder from the join.

8 To polish the ring either use a polishing wheel, a barrel polisher, or polishing attachments used on a drill (see page 131).

Rings decorated with wires.

Coloring metal wires

It is very satisfying to learn how to change the color of the metals you use. You can do this to wires that you are using in any context, not just when you are exploring the silversmithing techniques. It is important to check your information carefully before you start and follow all the safety instructions.

Oxidized silver chain.

Oxidizing silver

The purpose of oxidizing silver is to make the silver look darker than its traditional polished color. This can look particularly good on a textured surface which, once oxidized, is then polished to leave the darker color only in the indents. The technique can make an object look aged or give it more definition.

There are two main chemicals used to oxidize silver: one is called platinol and the other is liver of sulfur. You must take safety precautions when using both of them—wear rubber gloves, safety goggles, an apron, and a mask if possible. Also keep these chemicals out of the reach of children and don't eat or drink when you are using them.

TOOLS

1 Plastic gloves

2 Goggles

3 Apron

4 Mask

5 Brass wire brush

6 Paper towels

7 Paintbrush

8 Platinol

9 Liver of sulfur

10 Cold patination pre-treatment

11 Scopas Cupra

12 Wax or varnish to seal the verdigris

USING PLATINOL

This comes in a small plastic bottle as a black liquid and is the simpler of the two to use because it can be painted on straight from the bottle. It can also be used cold, unlike liver of sulfur.

1 Put on your safety equipment and read the instructions carefully. Polish the piece of silver that you want to oxidize first. Now make yourself a protected surface to work on with the paper towels.

2 With a paintbrush, paint the platinol all over the silver piece, or in selected areas. Platinol has a sulfurous base so it has a very unpleasant smell, like rotten eggs. This will instantly turn the silver black.

3 Leave the piece to dry for 10 minutes in a warm place.

4 Then repolish your piece to make the raised areas of the silver highly polished and leave the indented areas black.

USING LIVER OF SULFUR

This comes in a small plastic pot, in the form of small yellow nuggets. The advantage of liver of sulfur is that you can get a larger array of more subtle colors than the platinol, from yellows to blues and browns. The disadvantage is it has a much shorter shelf life and also needs to be heated up to work properly.

1 First put on safety equipment, prepare your work surface and read the instructions. Now polish the piece of silver to be colored.

2 Pour some hot water into a jam jar and drop a small nugget of liver of sulfur into it to dissolve—this will turn the water a yellowish color. The more you put in, the blacker the color you will get on the silver. If you make a weak solution you can get a wider range of colors.

AT-A-GLANCE SEQUENCE ▼

3 Run the piece of silver under a hot tap, since this helps the color change. Once the liver of sulfur has dissolved, place the silver into the jar. It is a good idea to hang it on a piece of string or wire so it is easier to get it out of the jar quickly.

4 Watch the piece of silver changing color and remove it from the jar when you like the color. Now run it under the cold tap to wash off the liver of sulfur solution and stop the color developing further. Dry the piece.

Examples of fused loops, colored with liver of sulfur.

Verdigris on copper

Verdigris produces a greenish tinge on copper, brass, or bronze. It has a matt, chalky finish and can produce a lovely aged effect. The type used here is a blue liquid that comes in a bottle and is called Scopas Cupra. It is an acid-based solution. Again, you must follow the safety precautions and read the instructions carefully. You will also need a cold patination pre-treatment solution.

1 Put on the recommended safety equipment and read the instructions. Take the piece to be verdigrized and clean it using a cold patination pre-treatment. This removes grease and dirt from the surface. You can rub it on with cotton wool or a rag. Leave it to dry.

2 Shake the bottle of Cupra, then paint it onto the metal surface. Leave it to dry in a warm place. You can apply several layers if you want to build up a stronger green color, but it can take several days for the color to build up.

3 When you are happy with the color, you must seal it with jade or a similar oil, or a clear wax. You can also try using a car varnish.

CHAPTER THREE
Gallery

The work of designers from around the world is featured in the gallery. You will recognize most of the techniques used and be able to see how they have been interpreted. Hopefully you will be inspired to create your own jewelry from the amazing varieties of wires and beads that are now available.

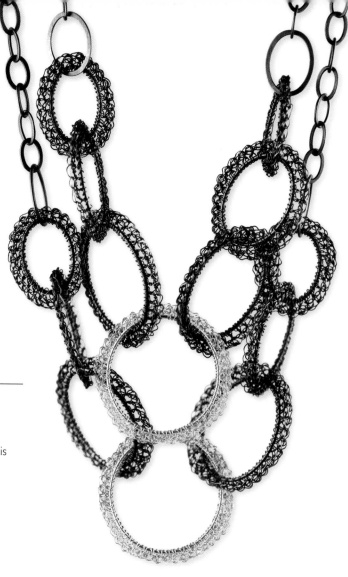

➤ Embellished Two-way Oval Necklace

TERI HOWES

These complicated loops have been hand-crocheted and then oxidized using silver, fine silver, and 18-carat gold wires. Then they have been looped together to make this extraordinary necklace.

◄ Wrist Mail

ELISE MANN

Four-link-wide basic flat chain-mail bracelet.

❯ Red Centre

LIZ REED

In this pendant, sterling silver wire and charms, gemstones, pearls, and Swarovski crystals have been worked together using weaving, shaping, hammering, and coiling. The end result has been oxidized to complete the very stylish effect.

◄ **The Seahorse**

HUAN PHAM

This intricate piece is made with a 14 mm Swarovski Rivoli, which is encased in silver wire and decorated with 2 mm silver beads to transform and enhance it.

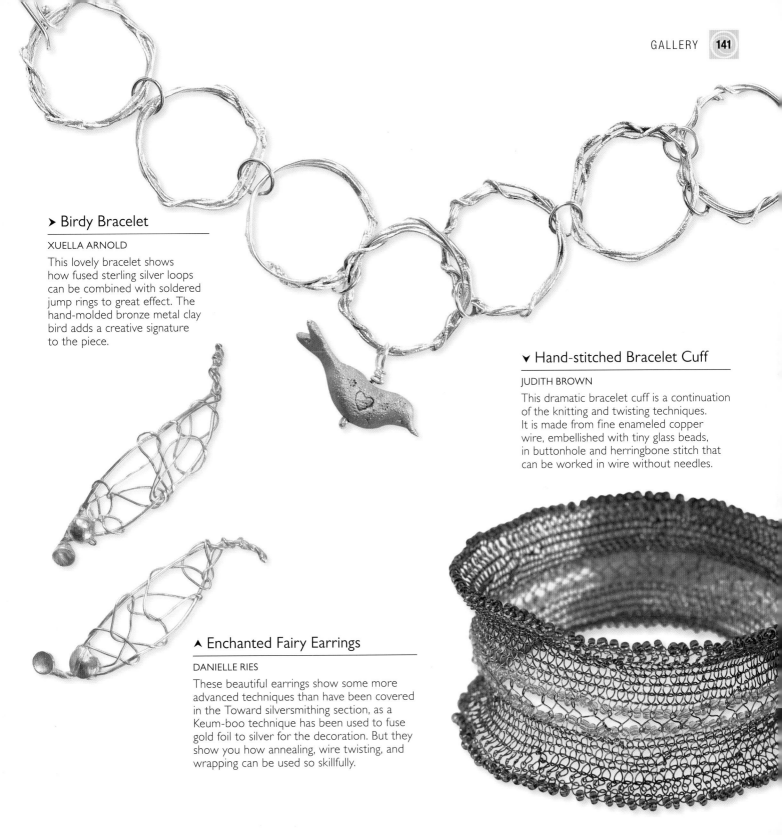

➤ Birdy Bracelet

XUELLA ARNOLD

This lovely bracelet shows how fused sterling silver loops can be combined with soldered jump rings to great effect. The hand-molded bronze metal clay bird adds a creative signature to the piece.

▼ Hand-stitched Bracelet Cuff

JUDITH BROWN

This dramatic bracelet cuff is a continuation of the knitting and twisting techniques. It is made from fine enameled copper wire, embellished with tiny glass beads, in buttonhole and herringbone stitch that can be worked in wire without needles.

▲ Enchanted Fairy Earrings

DANIELLE RIES

These beautiful earrings show some more advanced techniques than have been covered in the Toward silversmithing section, as a Keum-boo technique has been used to fuse gold foil to silver for the decoration. But they show you how annealing, wire twisting, and wrapping can be used so skillfully.

⏶ Glam Rock Multistrand

MONICA BOXLEY

This multistrand necklace consists of rock crystal and glass and metal beads strung irregularly onto wire to create a sumptuous rich effect. Each bead has the wire looped back through it to hold it securely in place.

⏶ Stepping-stones Weave Necklace

SARA READING

The artist has created a special weave to make this beautiful necklace with sterling silver jump rings.

➤ Twisted Circles Necklace

LINDA JONES

The chain units are created out of silver and copper wire that has been twisted together into a cable and then formed into figure-eight pieces, with the ends spiraled at the center. This design can be made with any color combination of wire, changing the diameters of the circular units by wrapping around various-sized mandrels.

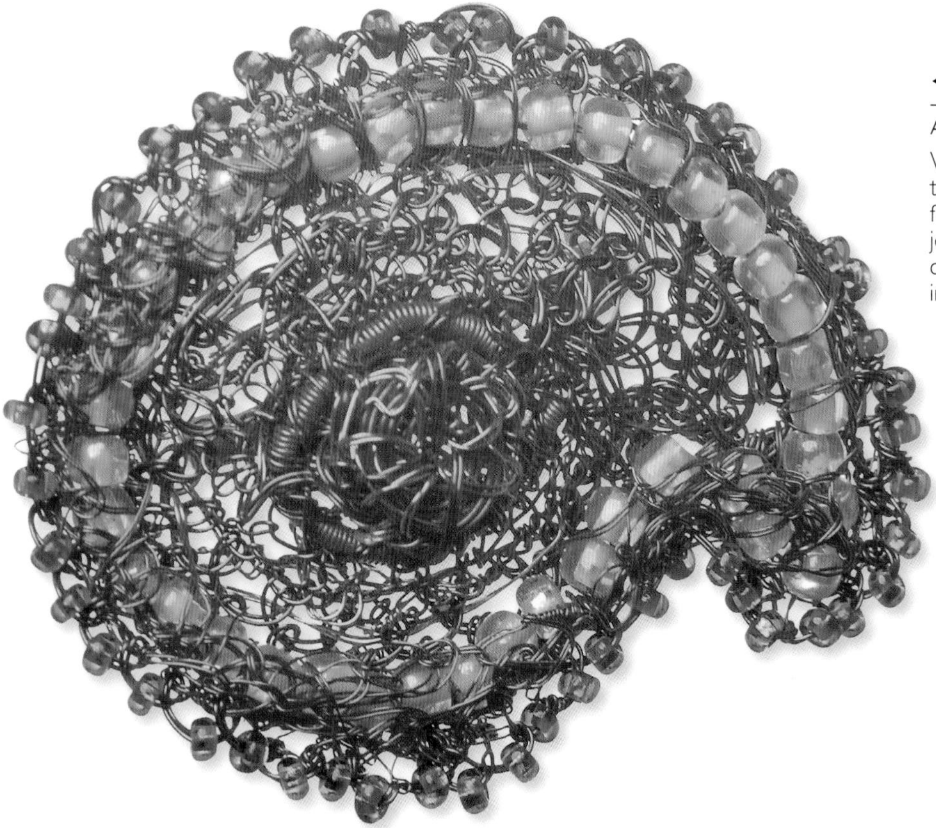

◄ **Paisley Brooch**

ALISON BAILEY SMITH

Wire reclaimed from old televisions has been randomly finger knotted and looped with jewelry-making wire and beads to create this unusual brooch. It even incorporates reused springs.

▼ **Knitted Necklace No. 3**

FIONA BARBER

This beautifully knitted necklace combines copper wire with lapis lazuli chips and glass beads.

➤ Chained Melody Necklace

LINDA JONES

This chain was created by the artist to demonstrate to her students all the different techniques that they had learned on a course. The wire shapes are linked with the blue beads to create a harmonious wire melody.

▾ Doodle Dangly Earrings

CHRISTINE KALTOFT

Lengths of 18 carat gold wire have been shaped, hammered, and soldered, and then joined with soldered jump rings to create stunning, fluid earrings.

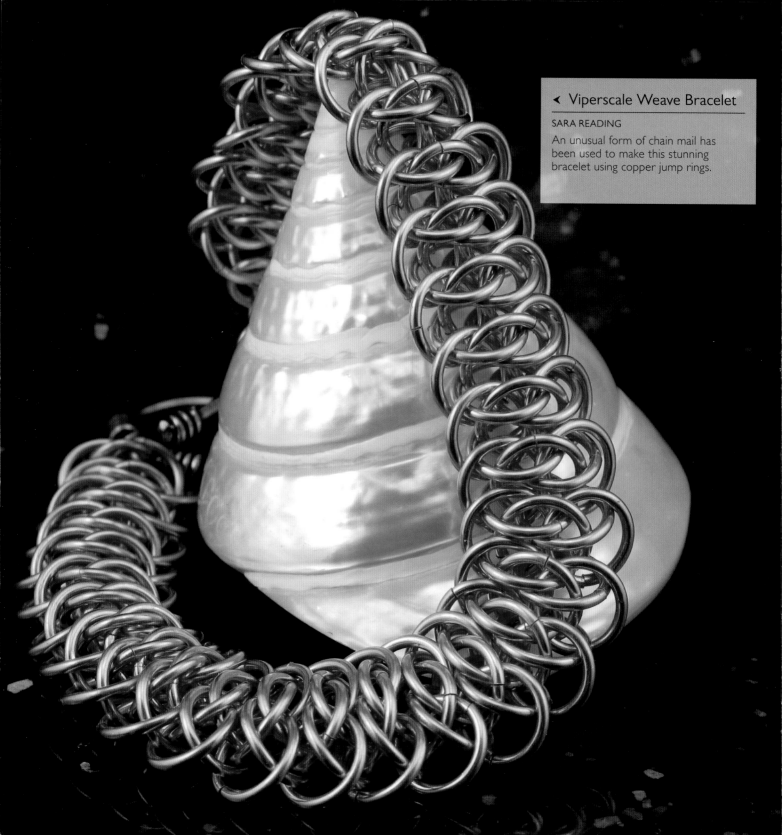

⌃ Embellished Hoop Earrings

TERI HOWES

These wonderful complex earrings have been hand crocheted in silver, fine silver, and 18 carat gold wire, and then oxidized.

➤ Avant Garde Ring

RACHEL ENTWISTLE

This exciting ring combines pearls and amethyst stones with enameled copper wire and silver wire.

➤ Bottle-top Bead Necklace

SARA WITHERS

A combination of recycled bottle tops and dichroic glass beads are linked together with coils and jump rings.

◄ Eye of Horus Bracelet

HUAN PHAM

This is a wirework Swarovski Rivoli crystal bangle, made from solid silver wire and gold-fill wire. It was constructed with half-hard 20 gauge (0.8 mm) wire to achieve a sturdy and strong construction. The central stone has been framed by the wires to form the bracelet and enhance its beauty.

➤ Knitted Wire Pod Necklaces

FIONA BARBER

The "pods" in these fascinating necklaces are hand knitted in copper wire with glass beads entwined. Then they are worked onto snake chains or bugle bead chains.

◄ Red and Black Collar

ALISON BAILEY SMITH

This stunning collar has been made with wire reclaimed from old televisions that has been randomly finger knotted. The wire is looped with feathers reclaimed from a fly-tying kit.

➤ Carnelain and Peridot Earrings

CHRIS POUPAZIS

Flat silver wire is skillfully curved into shape and then decorated with gems that are crimped onto beading wire.

➤ Colours of Autumn

MARYANNE VILLALBA

Brightly colored wires and Swarovski crystals have been worked together to create this wonderful neck piece.

➤ Love Hurts

ELLA HEIDI SAND

Beautifully shaped sterling silver wire is linked together to create an elegant necklace.

▲ Avant Garde Bangle

RACHEL ENTWISTLE

Silver and colored wires have been carefully combined with beautiful semiprecious stones to create this stunning bangle.

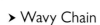

➤ Wavy Chain

LINDA JONES

This pretty chain has duplicated sections of curved silver wire linked together with beads and tiny figure-eight sections to keep it flexible. It is a wonderfully versatile chain, which will look completely different if made in different wires.

▲ Byzantine Star

ELISE MANN

Byzantine chain has been cleverly made into a star by connecting the groups to a central ring and adding glass bicone beads. This theme is continued into another chain to create a dramatic pendant.

› Tidal Pool

LIZ REED

To create this complex and beautiful work, sterling silver wire, and Thai hill tribe silver beads and charms have been combined with paua shell, Swarovski crystals, gemstones, and pearls. They have been woven, hammered, and combined with coils and the neck piece has been oxidized.

➤ Jewelled Sea

MARYANNE VILLALBA

This stunning neck piece is made with colored wire, Swarovski crystals, and seed beads. The wire has been shaped, wrapped, coiled, and hammered.

▲ Weaved Wire Shell

ERICA RUSSELL

A stunning pendant has been created by weaving silver wire to create a surround for a beautiful piece of shell.

◄ Turkish Mail Bracelet

SARAH AUSTIN

Turkish mail is also known as 3D Byzantine, or Byzantine worked in the round. In this stylish bracelet the mail has been made from enameled copper jump rings.

⌃ Wire Pendant

VERY GARCIA

Sterling silver jump rings were linked together in a chain mail method and looped together around a central jump ring, with a leather thong threaded through the outer hoops to create the pendant.

◄ Wirework Cocktail Ring

SIMON SCANTLEBURY

This bead ring was made with 26 gauge (0.4 mm) gold-plated copper wire. It was formed free-hand on a ring mandrel then lavishly wrapped with wire to create a glamorous effect.

Resources

SUPPLIERS

World of Beads
Via Murano
PO Box 1467
Castle Rock
CO 80104
www.viamurano.com

Wig Jig
PO Box 5124
Gaithersburg
MD 20882
www.wigjig.com

The Paramount Wire Company
2-8 Central Avenue
East Orange
NJ 07018
www.parawire.com

Beadworks
16 Redbridge Enterprise Centre
Thompson Close
Ilford,
Essex IG1 1TY
www.beadworks.co.uk
or www.beadworks.com

Beads Unlimited
PO Box 1, Hove
Sussex BN3 3SG
www.beadsunlimited.co.uk

Scientific Wire Company
18 Raven Road
South Woodford
London E18 1HW
www.wires.co.uk

Rashbel Marketing
24–28 Hatton Wall
London EC1N 8JH
www.rashbel.com

Beadsisters
07870 751833
www.beadsisters.co.uk

The Bead Scene Studio
Unit 4
Wakefield Lodge Estate
Pottersbury NN12 7QX
www.beadscene.com

BEAD SOCIETIES

There are bead societies in most U.S. states—just contact your local library for details. Alternatively, a quick Internet search will produce a list of possible societies and groups.

National Bead Society
3855 Lawrenceville Hwy,
Lawrenceville, GA 30044
Email: ibs@beadshows.com
www.nationalbeadsociety.com

The Bead Society of Greater Washington
The Jennifer Building
400 Seventh Street Northwest
Ground Floor
Washington, DC 20004
Email: info@bsgw.org

The Bead Society of Los Angeles
PO Box 241874
CA 90024
www.beadsocietyla.org

The Bead Society of Great Britain
c/o Carole Morris
1 Casburn Lane
Burwell
Cambs CB5 0ED
www.beadsociety.org.uk

The Beadworkers Guild
42–46 Lower Gravel Road
Bromley
Kent BR2 8LJ
T: +44 (0)20 8462 2625
www.beadworkersguild.org.uk

Crafts Council
44A Pentonville Road
London N1 9BY
www.craftscouncil.org.uk

The Bead Society of Victoria
PO Box 5312
Pinewood
Victoria 3149
www.beadsociety.com.au

PUBLICATIONS

Art Jewelry
www.artjewelrymag.com

Ornament
www.ornamentmagazine.com

WEBSITES

www.beadingdaily.com
www.enioken.com
www.jatayu.com
www.beadingforum.com.au

RING SIZES CHART

US	UK	Europe	mm	inches
½	A		37.83	1.490
¾	A ½		38.42	1.514
1	B		39.02	1.537
1 ¼	B ½		39.62	1.561
1 ½	C		40.22	1.585
1 ¾	C ½		40.82	1.608
2	D	1	41.42	1.632
2 ¼	D ½	2	42.02	1.655
2 ½	E		42.61	1.679
2 ¾	E ½	3	43.21	1.703
3	F	4	43.81	1.726
	F ½		44.41	1.750
3 ¼	G	5	45.01	1.773
3 ½	G ½		45.61	1.797
3 ¾	H	6	46.20	1.820
4	H ½		46.80	1.844
4 ¼	I	7	47.40	1.868
4 ½	I ½	8	48.00	1.891
4 ¾	J		48.60	1.915
5	J ½	9	49.20	1.938
5 ¼	K	10	49.80	1.962
5 ½	K ½		50.39	1.986
5 ¾	L	11	50.99	2.009
6	L ½		51.59	2.033
6 ¼	M	12	52.19	2.056
6 ½	M ½	13	52.79	2.080
6 ¾	N		53.47	2.107
	N ½	14	54.10	2.132
7	O	15	54.74	2.157
7 ¼	O ½		55.38	2.182
7 ½	P	16	56.02	2.207
7 ¾	P ½		56.66	2.232
8	Q	17	57.30	2.257
8 ¼	Q ½	18	57.94	2.283
8 ½	R		58.57	2.308
8 ¾	R ½	19	59.21	2.333
9	S	20	59.85	2.358
9 ¼	S ½		60.49	2.383
9 ½	T	21	61.13	2.408
9 ¾	T ½	22	61.77	2.434
10	U		62.40	2.459
10 ¼	U ½	23	63.04	2.484
10 ½	V	24	63.68	2.509
10 ¾	V ½		64.32	2.534
11	W	25	64.88	2.556
11 ¼	W ½		65.48	2.580
11 ½	X	26	66.07	2.603
11 ¾	X ½		66.67	2.627
12	Y		67.27	2.650
12 ¼	Y ½		67.87	2.674
12 ½	Z		68.47	2.680

WIRE GAUGE CHART

Gauge	Size in SWG	Size in AWG
16	1.63mm	1.30mm
18	1.22mm	1.02mm
20	0.91mm	0.81mm
21*	0.81mm	0.73mm
22	0.71mm	0.63mm
24	0.55mm	0.50mm
26	0.45mm	0.40mm
28	0.37mm	0.32mm
30	0.31mm	0.25mm

*This gauge of wire is often used to make earwires.

Index

Acknowledgments

Quarto would like to thank the following for kindly supplying images for inclusion in this book:

p.138t, 147t Teri Howes www.terihowesjewellery.com
p.138b, 152br Elise Mann
p.139, 153 Liz Reed
p.140, 148b Huan Pham www.huanpham.blogspot.com
p.141t Xuella Arnold www.xuella.co.uk
p.141mr Judith Brown www.judithbrownjewellery.co.uk
p.141b Danielle Ries danielle.ries@btinternet.com
p.142tl Monica Boxley www.monicaboxley.co.uk
p.142tr, 146 Sara Reading of Corvus Chainmaille www.flickr.com/photos/redcrow
p.143, 145r, 152bl Linda Jones www.wirejewellery.co.uk
p.144t, 150t Alison Bailey Smith www.abscraft.com
p.144b, 149 Fiona Barber www.fe-b-jewellery.co.uk
p.145bl Christine Kaltoft www.christinekaltoft.co.uk
p.147b, 152t Rachel Entwistle www.rachelentwistle.co.uk
p.148t Sara Withers www.sarawithers.co.uk
p.150b Chris Poupazis
p.151b, 154t Maryanne Villalba
p.151b Ella Heidi Sand www.heidisand.com
p.154bl Erica Russell
p.154br Sarah Austin www.beadsisters.co.uk
p.155t Very Garcia www.verygarcia.co.uk
p.155b Simon Scantlebury/World of Beads
www.worldofbeads.co.uk

While every effort has been made to
credit contributors, Quarto would
like to apologize should there have been
any omissions or errors—and would
be pleased to make the appropriate
correction for future editions of the book.